A FIFTH GOSPEL

JOSEPH G. HEALEY, M.M. (Maryknoll) is currently engaged in spiritual formation and missionary spirituality programs at Maryknoll Seminary. Fr. Healey has spent ten years in Africa. During his last two years there, he lived and worked in Nyabihanga Ujamaa village in Tanzania. Previously he was Social Communications Secretary of the Association of Member Episcopal Conferences in Eastern Africa (AMECEA) for five years. He holds degrees in philosophy, theology and journalism, and is the author of numerous articles.

A FIFTH GOSPEL

The Experience of Black
Christian Values

Joseph G. Healey

ORBIS BOOKS

Maryknoll, New York 10545

Copyright © 1981 Orbis Books, Maryknoll NY 10545
All rights reserved
Manufactured in the United States of America

Library of Congress Cataloging in Publication Data

Healey, Joseph.
  A fifth Gospel.

  1. Catholic Church in Eastern Africa.
2. Catholic Church—Missions—Africa, Eastern.
3. Africa, Eastern—Religion. 4. Healey,
Joseph. 5. Missions—Africa, Eastern. I. Title.
BX1680.5.H4   282'.678   80-25033
ISBN 0-88344-013-X (pbk.)

To the Christians of Nyabihanga and Bukiriro villages
in Tanzania, especially Bishop Christopher Mwoleka,
who have shared with me so deeply and taught me so much

Contents

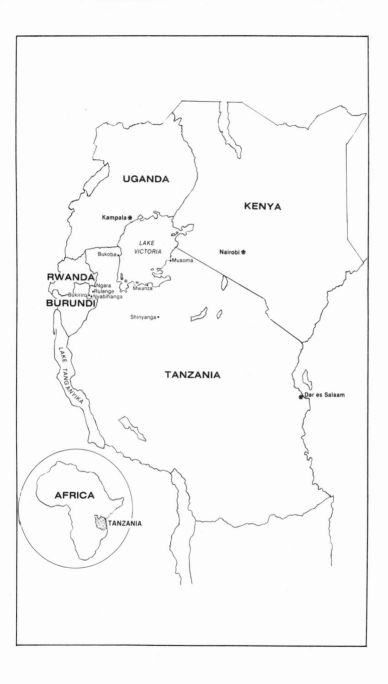

Foreword

Joseph Healey is a young American who has lived ten years in Africa. This is his story, the outward journey of a traveler and the inner journey of a pilgrim. The more he traveled the deeper grew his conviction that the real journey in life is the inner journey. As he puts it, "the inner journey of the spirit . . . is the longest and most important journey of our lives. It is a pilgrimage of the heart."

Father Healey went to Africa as a Maryknoll Missioner of the so-called new breed: " 'The greatest good we can do for others is not just to share our riches with them but to reveal their riches to themselves.' Missionaries do not bring the Christian faith or religion or truth to Africa. Christ is already present in the African people, working in his mysterious ways. The missionary's role is to help the African people to discover the active presence of Christ in their lives. . . ." Healey went to Africa "not as a bringer or giver, but as a receiver; . . . not as a teacher, but as a learner; not as a leader, but as a servant." He was privileged "to participate in the Africans' rendezvous with destiny, their discovery of their own Christian identity and authenticity." As Fr. Healey quotes Bishop Peter Sarpong of Ghana, ". . . if Christianity's claim to be universal is to be believed, then it is not Africa that must be Christianized, but Christianity that must be Africanized."

Father Healey deeply recognized that "we were on a search together—a search for meaning in life, a search for the best ways to respond to Christ's call in our lives. As a fellow searcher, I would at times challenge the Africans and they would challenge me. And so we would grow together."

Healey's ten years in Africa witnessed a remarkable growth of Christianity. Sheer numbers can be deceptive and misleading but the increase is impressive.

	1968	1978
Christians	75 million	120 million
Catholics	30 million	51 million
African Cardinals	5	12
African Bishops	115	239
African Priests	3355	5034

The most distinctive and fascinating part of this book covers Father Healey's two years in a *Ujamaa* ("Familyhood") village, where animating small Christian communities was his main pastoral work. Here he lived and shared the daily life of the ordinary people. Here we meet the extraordinary African bishop Christopher Mwoleka and his dream of a new Christian community being realized.

"Evangelical poverty" becomes a decision to live simply in the midst of plenty. "Presence ministry" is to work not *for* but *with* people, a total being with people, a oneness with them that is beyond expectations. The simple phenomenon of African rain opens up a new depth to the ministry of uncertainty and the ministry of insecurity.

The small Christian communities demand a spirituality of communal relationships and a new gospel experience of living for others. Father Healey has listened well to his African brothers and sisters. His journal is filled with marvelous stories and proverbs. My favorite is "When elephants fight, the grass gets hurt." This book is an "apocalypse"—an uncovering of the continent that still remains dark and little known to most Americans. It is a revelation of what the Holy Spirit is doing in one of the most dynamic areas of the Christian church today. This is a prophetic book, an invitation and a call to what the future can be. Father Joseph Healey's journey opens up new possibilities for discovering and recognizing the hidden richness of the black church in the United States "that has been with us for so long a time and we still do not know it." Here is a contemporary experience of our forgotten roots.

When Father Healey left his *Ujamaa* village in Tanzania, a close friend thanked him for "embracing the life of us Africans at its roots." Readers of this book will add an "Amen" to these words of simple gratitude.

In 1980 Father Joseph Healey spent ten days at St. Agnes Parish in Detroit, Michigan, giving us a week-long retreat on "African Christian Values and the Small Christian Communities." Tanzania came to Detroit and stirred up possibilities that had never before been awakened. What developed out of this experience is the realization that African Christian values are universal values and have a special significance in industrial Detroit. Even though these are countercultural values, this exposure and involvement is generating an excitement over the gifts and challenges that Africa has to offer the Christian tradition and the world. New models of liturgy, community, and ministry have been witnessed, and an invitation has been felt to rediscover and reinterpret the black heritage and tradition. This may well be a new answer to the secular anguish of our Western culture.

Rev. Edward J. Farrell

Preface

During ten years in East Africa I experienced again and again the African value that sharing is a way of life. After the African people* have shared so deeply with me I feel compelled to share my experience in Africa with people in other parts of the world. My experience is not important for its own sake alone but as a bridge, a link to African peoples and cultures.

The real authors of this book are the African people. I have tried to let them speak for themselves and their values: the prophetic Bishop Christopher Mwoleka, the Catholic bishops of Eastern Africa,** the visionary President Julius Nyerere, the old farmer Patrice, the catechist Astheria, the schoolboys Thomas and Christopher, and the small Christian communities in Nyabihanga and Bukiriro villages in western Tanzania. This is their story as much as it is mine.

Their story is the story of a young socialistic country struggling to become self-reliant, a fast growing Catholic church slowly developing an African identity, grassroots Christian communities creating a new approach to evangelization, and African traditions and customs taking on new meaning. There is an African proverb: "I pointed out to you the moon and all you saw was my finger." Regretfully I realize that a non-African can get *inside* the African experience only so far, yet I have tried to be faithful to the African way. My African friends can tell me whether I have glimpsed the African moon or only an African finger.

In my African pilgrimage I started as a Western missionary and ended as a fellow searcher with the African people. In learning about and sharing the African way I have experienced it as teacher

* When I use the words "Africa" and "African," I am referring mainly to my experience in Eastern Africa.

**"Eastern Africa" in this book refers to the ecclesiastical division of the Catholic church that includes Ethiopia, Kenya, Malawi, Sudan, Tanzania, Uganda, and Zambia.

and as friend. Experiencing the richness of African Christian values and African Christianity has meant entering into a narrative theology of inculturation. In the process I have learned much from Africa's Fifth Gospel. Just as North America, Latin America, Europe, and Asia have their unique Fifth Gospels so God is revealing himself today through the African people within their local environment.

African Christianity offers a unique contribution to the universal church and the whole world. In sharing my experience of the African way I hope that these African Christian values will challenge other cultures, especially Western society. Such African values as community, personal relationships, sharing, waiting, joint responsibility, and service prophetically question Western culture, which is increasingly blinded by materialism, consumerism, and individualism.

Also I hope that this book can be a bridge between Africa and the West, between Africa and other Third World countries and churches, between Africa and the universal church. We have much to learn and to share in dialogue with each other.

If you read this book as a romantic trip to some far-off land, you may escape the often uncomfortable questions that certain African Christian values raise. If, however, you enter into the African experience, you may discover a message and a way of life that can give new meaning to the universal church and the whole world.

I
A Search in Africa

Morning mist lifts from the hills and valleys of Nyabihanga village in Western Tanzania. Villagers walk to the nearby fields to cultivate beans, corn, and millet. Banana trees shelter the simple homes that are hardly visible as one looks over the hills. African farmers are close to nature's life cycle.

Three neighbors in Nyabihanga, Mattias, Dorothea, and Angelina, express the curiosity and wonder of Tanzanian children. The extended families in the village are an ideal natural environment for the development of small Christian communities.

Bishop Christopher Mwoleka inspects our small farm in Nyabihanga village with Athanasius Misambo, Joseph Mukasa, and myself. We tried to live a ministry of spiritual presence by sharing the everyday life of the Tanzanian people on the grassroots level.

My First Mission Journey

It was August 1968. The place was Tarime, Tanzania, on the Tanzania–Kenya border. I had arrived in northern Tanzania with two other Maryknoll priests after an eight-hour drive from Nairobi.

This was my first visit to Musoma Diocese, where Maryknoll's missionary work in Africa had begun twenty-two years earlier. Now I too had come to Tanzania to begin my own missionary work. It was my first mission journey. I was very eager to reach Tarime Parish, the first parish on the road south from the border. I couldn't wait to walk around the compound and get the feel of the Africa I had come to serve. . . .

I walked into the back of the simple, yet dignified church. Two Africans were silently praying. I felt deeply moved to be with them—at this time, in this place. In a very real sense I felt I had come to join these two Africans and all their people to search and to share together. I felt very happy to be reaching out toward the future with them.

As I sat in the back of that Tarime church I thought about this first journey to Africa and my missionary vocation. I looked again at the two Africans silently praying. I thought of a quotation I had heard: "The greatest good we can do for others is not just to share our riches with them but to reveal their riches to themselves." Missionaries do not bring the Christian faith or religion or truth to Africa. Christ is already present in the African people, working in his mysterious ways. The missionary's role is to help the African people to discover the active presence of Christ in their lives, to be more conscious of his healing and saving power, and to detect the riches of their own culture and way of life in order to integrate them into Christianity. This sort of approach is far removed from any kind of ecclesiastical colonialism or any imposition of Western forms of Christianity on Africa. In this connection a quotation from Bishop Peter Sarpong of Ghana is apropos: "For if Christianity's claim to be universal is to be believed, then it is not Africa that must be Christianized, but Christianity that must be Africanized."

I was coming to Africa not as a bringer or giver, but as a receiver (and, ideally, a sharer); not as a teacher, but as a learner; not as a leader, but as a servant. I was privileged to participate in the Africans' rendezvous with destiny: their discovery of their own Christian identity and authenticity. We were on a search together—a search for meaning in life, a search for the best ways to respond to Christ's call in our lives. As a fellow searcher, I would at times challenge the Africans and they would challenge me. And so we would grow together.

Reflecting on this first journey to Africa I thought of other missionary journeys in the history of the church: the call of Abraham when Yahweh said to him: "Leave your country, your family and your father's house, for the land I will show you" (Gen. 12:1).* I remembered the call of Isaiah when the voice of the Lord said: "Whom shall I send? Who will be our messenger?" And Isaiah answered: "Here I am, send me" (Isa. 6:8-9). I recalled how our Lord Jesus Christ had sent out the eleven apostles to "make disciples of all the nations," giving them some of the most consoling and strengthing words in the whole Bible: "And know that I am with you always; yes, to the end of time" (Matt. 28:19-20).

The journeys of many great missionaries flashed through my mind: Saint Paul tirelessly traveling the length and breadth of Asia Minor; Saint Francis Xavier reaching out to India and Japan; the Holy Ghost Fathers landing at Bagamoyo in 1868—the first modern missionaries to set foot on East African soil; the pioneering White Fathers (Missionaries of Africa) fearlessly entering what are now Tanzania and Uganda in 1878-79; Maryknoll's first band of missionary priests setting out for China in 1918. And here was I, in 1968 among the new missionaries following this great tradition. It made me feel humble and small. Yet I believed in the depth of my heart that Christ's promise to his first missionary disciples was a promise to me as well: "I am with you always; yes, to the end of time."

As I began my mission life, I reflected at length on what I call

---

*Biblical quotations are from the Jerusalem Bible, unless specified otherwise.

"journey theology." There are many "theologies" in the church today: liberation theology, political theology, theology of hope, radical theology, black theology, story theology, process theology. I have often wondered why no one has written about journey theology. The theme of journey—and its related meanings, such as search, exploration, pilgrimage—is a rich and fruitful theme in literature. The many journey books and novels, such as the *Aeneid, The Canterbury Tales, Gulliver's Travels, Pilgrims Progress, Don Quixote, Huckleberry Finn, Portrait of the Artist as a Young Man, and Lord of the Rings*, have captured the imagination of humankind. Mostly, there is the portrait of a lonely hero always searching, always striving, always launching out into the deep. In other writings the hero is the traveler, the wanderer, the wonderer, the person on the road. The road may be a spatial one (travels around the world), a social one (a dialogue with others), a spiritual one (an inner journey) or, best, a combination of all three. A person's search for meaning is as old as Abraham going forth to a new land, and as contemporary as the euphoria of drug-induced experiences.

Within all of us is the eternal quest to discover who we are, and what the meaning of life is. The Christian response is that life indeed has meaning—a meaning found in human beings themselves and in their loving relationship to God their Creator and Father. Journey theology is therefore fundamental to the Christian life. Always central is the pilgrimage theme: human beings traveling on earth seeking the eternal life that actually begins here and now. Closely related is the importance of the kingdom of God, which is already here and yet is still coming.

All this is summed up in a section from the Vatican II document *Lumen gentium* (Dogmatic Constitution on the Church). The chapter heading "The Eschatological Nature of the Pilgrim Church" sounds erudite, but essentially it emphasizes that we are a pilgrim people, a wayfaring church. We are on the road, in process. We haven't arrived yet, so we don't have all the answers. This should help our humility and simplicity. As good travelers we shouldn't take too much baggage (a mistake often made by the institutional church with all its "trappings"). We should travel light and be flexible. We should also travel confidently in the Spirit.

Journey theology tells us that from the beginning of time God our loving Father has planned our final destination. In and through our Lord Jesus Christ we can move toward the Parousia, his final coming in glory; for we are all traveling on the road to salvation. Jesus Christ has saved us and redeemed us by his cross and resurrection. But we must constantly be renewed, reformed, and undergo a conversion of heart.

Looking at the small percentage of Christians within the total world population, we have indeed taken the road "less traveled by." It is not an easy road. And yet it is very easy. This is the paradox of following Christ, of responding to his call to love, sacrifice, and service. Sometimes the road is rocky. At other times it is poorly marked. At times we just want to sit by the roadside, out of the flow of traffic. But we realize that the Christian commitment is to continue steadfastly on our journey despite the hot sun, our tired feet, our heavy burdens. We realize that Christ experienced this same heat, this same tiredness, these same burdens, first when he walked the way of the cross on Good Friday; now as he shares in the struggles of every man, woman, and child in their journey through life.

On this journey a special help for us is a "spirituality of the road"—a spirituality for the Christian traveler. To meet Christ and to be helped by the strength that only he can give, we have at times to go into the desert; at other times we have to go up the mountain. It is significant that the Old Testament prophets met Yahweh in a special way in the desert and on the mountaintop. Here too is where Christ was in deepest communion with his heavenly Father. In the history of the Christian saints and mystics, the desert and the mountain have been favorite meeting places of God and his creatures. Here in some mysterious way we come to learn that the longest journey is the inner journey, the journey of the spirit, where we meet God in the silence of our hearts.

Still another meeting place of God and ourselves is among the poor, the suffering, the lonely, the forgotten, the little people. Jesus tells us that we discover him, we meet him, we touch him through his poor, through his persecuted, through his oppressed.

This journey theology, or theology for a pilgrim, says a great deal about the Christian vocation, the missionary vocation, and relationships with the African people. We are all searchers together, fellow travelers on the road. From my first coming to Africa, I became increasingly a part of the journey of the African people and the African church. It was and continues to be an exciting and surprising journey in the Spirit.

After my first journey to that small church in Tarime, Tanzania, I continued on to Musoma, where I studied Swahili for four months in the Maryknoll Language School. Language study completed, I left Tanzania to live in Nairobi, Kenya, doing social communications work for the Catholic Bishops of AMECEA (Association of Member Episcopal Conferences in Eastern Africa). For six years I traveled around Africa, visiting many countries and returning to Tanzania many times. During these pilgrim years I began searching for my real home in Africa, in Tanzania. Without my being aware of it, events and circumstances began taking place, preparing me for a special journey—the journey to Nyabihanga.

A Spiritual Pilgrimage

In July 1972 I made a private retreat in Kajiado, which is about fifty miles from Nairobi. The retreat house is connected with a Fraternity of the Little Sisters of Jesus. These days of prayer and silence started a process, or better, awakened a process of understanding what I felt God was calling me to do and to be. I had always been attracted to the spirituality of Charles de Foucauld. Now, rereading books by his desciple, René Voillaume, I was inspired anew to a vocation similar to that of the Little Brothers and the Little Sisters, who combine an intense spiritual life with an intense active life. Voillaume describes the life of the Little Brothers as a life totally present to God in prayer, and to men and women in poverty and love.

I also began reflecting about the inspiring life of Mother Teresa of Calcutta. In an interview she described the big decision in her life: to leave the vocation of teaching in order to live and work among the poorest of the poor. She spoke of "a call within my vocation. It was a second calling. It was a vocation to give up even

Loreto, where I was very happy, and to go out in the streets to serve the poorest of the poor."

Gradually I began reflecting deeply about a second calling, a call within a call, in my own missionary vocation. This new call developed in two ways: toward a more contemplative way of life, and toward a deeper sharing in the life of the poor and simple people on the local level. More and more I felt called to be a "contemplative in the world," among the Tanzanian people in a small *Ujamaa* (Swahili for "Familyhood") village. This would be a ministry of spiritual presence, a ministry of "being" more than "doing."

The six years (1968–74) that I worked as Social Communications Secretary of AMECEA in Nairobi were happy ones. Especially enjoyable was the opportunity to coordinate communications training programs for African priests, Sisters, and lay people. But in 1973 and 1974, as I prepared to turn over the communications work to Father Joseph Mukwaya, a Ugandan priest, I began praying and reflecting more about God's second call to me, trying to discern the direction my missionary vocation would take after my work with AMECEA would be completed. What was Christ calling me to be and to do during the next part of my missionary life? How could I imitate Christ more completely? How could prayer and community life become a more important part of my missionary vocation? The gospel confronted me with some challenging questions. Why does Jesus say: "Go and sell everything you own and give the money to the poor, and you will have treasures in heaven; then come, follow me" (Mark 10:21)? Why does the Son of man have "no place to lay his head"? Why does Christ have "to suffer and die" before he enters into his glory? How do we follow Christ's command to "go out to the whole world; proclaim the Good News to all creation" (Mark 16:16)?

Discerning these questions in relation to my own missionary vocation led me on a spiritual pilgrimage around the world from December 1974 to November 1975. I wanted to search "in the Spirit" for the vocation within a vocation in my own life.

In my travels I discovered that throughout the world priests, Brothers, Sisters, laymen, and laywomen are responding to the call to live a ministry of presence among the people: on sugar plantations in Central America; in the slums of New York; on the waterfront of Marseilles; in the factories of Hong Kong. This call is to the Church of the Poor, the Church of the Working Class, the Church of the "Little People."

I felt that my call was to Africa and specifically to a small rural village in Tanzania. At present the philosophy of *Ujamaa*, Tanzanian socialism, the Arusha Declaration (1967; defining African socialism), and the rapid growth of *Ujamaa* villages and *Maendeleo* ("Development") villages provide a unique opportunity for the church to be one with the people in the development of community living and teamwork, in self-reliance, and in working for progress and a better quality of life in all its dimensions.

Along with this call to the presence ministry among the people on the local level in Tanzania, my spiritual journey led me to discover the importance of "small Christian communities" (hereafter referred to as SCCs)—Christians living, sharing, praying, working, and witnessing together in a neighborhood group.* I felt called to live in an SCC in Tanzania and to try to live the gospel values on the local, grassroots level.

My spiritual pilgrimage was as much an inner journey as it was a physical trip around the world. In the silence of an encounter with God in my heart, I tried to discover the direction in which the Spirit was leading me.

First I made a three-week walking pilgrimage through the Holy Land to get a real feeling for the historical events in Jesus' life and in the life of the early church. I had one major purpose: to visit the holy places of Jesus' life and retrace his steps, to meditate on the most important passages in the New Testament, and to reflect on what all this means for our world today. I focused on the events of Jesus' life in chronological order, spending three days in Bethlehem, three days in Nazareth, three days around the Jordan River and Jericho, and six days in Jerusalem. This gave plenty of time for quiet meditation and reflection on the life and times of Jesus. Each day I celebrated the Eucharist at a church or shrine commemorating an important event in Jesus' life. I read slowly and meditatively the relevant gospel passages, and gradually the pro-

*The development, growth, and everyday life of SCCs are described below, pp. 37–43, 98–149.

found meaning of the Holy Land became a deeper part of my Christian experience. My purpose was to meet the person of Jesus Christ in a new and deeper way, to experience the Bible as God's living Word, and to discover the active presence of God working in and through his people today. All this deepened the motivation for my future "contemplative-in-the-world" vocation in Tanzania.

A thirty-day directed retreat in Poona, India, gave me a valuable Third World context for my prayer and discernment. Two parts of this retreat stand out in my mind and heart. First, the retreat was a real experience of God on a deeper level than I had ever experienced before. One Indian Jesuit said to me, "In the West to know God is *to know about God* (the intellectual, rational, mental approach). But in India to know God is *to experience God* (the intuitive, feeling, heart approach)." I discovered this for myself, experiencing contemplative prayer (silent union prayer, quiet, affective prayer) on a regular basis for the first time in my life. This kind of prayer does away with intellectual activity, images, and thoughts. It is a "being prayer" rather than a "doing prayer," and it intensified my spiritual consciousness and my awareness of the active presence of God in my life.

The second highlight of the retreat was the discernment process. I discovered that discernment was deeper than analysis and reflection, and that it enabled me to discover more clearly God's plan for me. During the thirty days I asked: How can I live a more prayerful life? What kind of ministry of spiritual presence is God calling me to? I found that answers came when I opened myself to the guidance of the Holy Spirit.

Once again taking up my travels, I discovered that the riches of Eastern spirituality have great relevance for spirituality in Africa. Next, in the United States, I learned about the charismatic movement and lived in a house of prayer. A further high point of my spiritual pilgrimage was the opportunity to live with the Little Brothers of the Gospel, first in New York City, and later in three places in Cameroon, West Africa. This was a firsthand experience of an integration of contemplative and active dimensions of life. Conversations with the Little Brothers about building and deepening community life were deeply valuable as I prepared to live a community life mainly with Africans in Tanzania.

As I review the experiences I had during my eleven-month spiritual pilgrimage, four themes or priorities stand out: (1) *Abandonment to God:* Again and again the call came to give myself more completely to God and to let God work in and through me. (2) *Spirituality of the Heart:* I experienced the transition from an intellectual approach to a more affective approach in my whole life. A rigid, legalistic mentality gradually gave way to a more flexible, human outlook. This heart-over-head emphasis influenced my prayer life, my personal relationships, and my lifestyle. I became more person-centered than task-oriented. Being was more important than doing. (3) *Experience of God:* My many spiritual-renewal experiences seemed linked to a living experience of God. The experience of contemplative prayer, the experience of spiritual presence in everyday life, "experiential Christianity" rather than institutional Christianity, and living, praying communities are some examples. (4) *Spiritual Growth in Community:* Some of my most meaningful experiences came from being part of "praying communities." Community support was essential in my own growth. This included sharing my spiritual experiences with close friends and participating in spiritual presence as a community witness.

Once my spiritual pilgrimage was over, I returned to Tanzania and began living a "contemplative-in-the-world" vocation as a Maryknoller. In Rulenge Diocese in western Tanzania, in the village of Nyabihanga, I was able to evolve the right blend of contemplation and active ministry, of spiritual presence and work among the people, of being and doing.

Conversation at the Ferry

To reach my chosen village of Nyabihanga I had to travel by car, by bus, and then by car again. In Mwanza, Tanzania, on the southeastern shore of Lake Victoria, I met Bishop Christopher Mwoleka, the bishop of the Catholic Diocese of Rulenge. In his Land-Rover we drove west for 235 miles to reach Rulenge town. The actual driving time was about nine hours on a bumpy dirt road.

Outside Mwanza we had to wait for an hour and a half for the Kigongo–Busisi Ferry, a delay that gave us an opportunity for discussing possible attitudes towards waiting. In summary: (1) give way to impatience, frustration, or annoyance at the delay; the one-and-a-half-hour wait is just a waste of time; (2) fill up the time as "usefully" as possible: read a book, write letters, talk to a friend; (3) share the wait with the people around as part of the "ministry of waiting," an example of the "ministry of spiritual presence."

On the Kigongo–Busisi Ferry cars were given preference over buses and trucks. On the day we crossed, truck drivers had to wait up to five hours before crossing. During the harvest season trucks loaded with cotton have to wait as much as two days before crossing. Women with babies in their arms sometimes have to wait for three days at the bus station before getting a bus from Mwanza to Bukoba, a distance of 270 miles. During the school holiday season there could even be a two-week wait to get a bus for this journey.

But waiting was not always concerned with traveling. The people had to wait an enormous length of time at hospitals, dispensaries, and village health centers. Once as I myself sat for a long time waiting to see the doctor at the hospital, I saw streams of pregnant women and gaunt old men waiting in line. I knew that early that morning they had come on foot in the hot sun, some of them walking for two or three hours. They would make the same journey back again in the afternoon, and as I waited with them, I knew that they were more patient than I was.

So, on this day at the ferry, Bishop Christopher and I talked about all these waiting situations. We realized that as persons with cars, as persons with quick access to medicine and hospital attention, we escape many of the cares and uncertainties of the people we live near. Yet we knew the "waiting ministry" to be an important part of the Christian vocation. In various kinds of waiting situations we can identify with the people in their hardships and sufferings. We can try to be one with them in the uncertainty and endlessness of their waiting.

Always with waiting comes patience. There is a Swahili proverb that says "Patience is the key to tranquillity." One of the modern translations of the New Testament puts a section of the Epistle of

Saint James this way: "For when the way is rough, your patience has a chance to grow. So let it grow, and don't try to squirm out of your problems. For when your patience is finally full bloom, then you will be ready for anything, strong in character, full and complete" (James 1:2–4). In his Epistle to the Romans, Saint Paul links suffering and patience: ". . . we can boast about our sufferings. These sufferings bring patience, as we know, and patience brings perseverance, and perseverance brings hope . . ." (Rom. 5:3–4). So there is meaning in waiting. It is not just wasting time. Many times I have seen how Africans really enjoy waiting. It fits into their leisurely pace of living, and emphasizes personal relationships more than the accomplishment of tasks. Waiting gives them a chance to talk with friends and to catch up on the local news. They are not concerned about the ticking of the clock, the minutes that are passing. Waiting in itself is an experience of life.

But the ministry of waiting is especially hard when there are many tasks to be done. Then comes the temptation to impatience. Time-conscious, we worry about all the work that has to be done. We don't have time to wait. So a heavily task-oriented life can jar with the waiting ministry. Yet we must learn to wait and, ideally, to enjoy waiting. With the patience of waiting comes an inner peace and harmony.

For many people waiting is tolerable—if success eventually comes. We can put up with waiting if it finally brings results: if the ferry comes, or if a bus with empty seats stops, or if the needed medicine is available. But in Tanzania and in many other places I have visited, a long wait does not guarantee success. A bus may finally come, but it may be full. After reaching the front of a long line at the dispensary, a mother may find that the right medicine for her sick child is not in stock. Here is an opportunity for the real waiting ministry: sharing the experience of the people when the waiting is in vain, or fruitless, and we hear "Sorry, no room" or "Come back tomorrow."

A special way of sharing with the people is to travel by bus. To get a car ride is to avoid the uncertainties and unpredictableness of ordinary travel: pushing and shoving in line before buying a ticket, waiting at the bus stop, standing for part or all of the trip, constantly checking that one's bags are still on the overhead rack, experiencing a growing thirst on a hot, dry day when a bottle of soda or clean water is not available.

Traveling by bus in Tanzania brings an endless succession of delays, changes of timetable, breakdowns, missed connections, waiting. Once I went by bus from Rulenge to Katerere village to visit the Maryknoll Sisters. A car can make the trip in one and a quarter hours. The forty-mile journey took me thirteen and a quarter hours. First there was a three-hour wait in Rulenge for the bus to arrive. Then came a three-hour bus ride on a bumpy dirt road. Afterward there was a three-hour wait for the noonday sun to go down, since walking in the middle of the day can be very, very hot. A further two-hour delay was caused by waiting for the customary afternoon rain to stop. Finally there was a two-and-a-quarter-hour walk from the main road down into the valley to reach Katerere village. At another time I might have found this hard, but on this day it was meaningful because I was sharing the everyday experience of the people.

Though traveling by bus can be a way of sharing with the people it can be a luxury at times. Often people don't have enough money for a bus ticket. Again in many areas of Tanzania there are no buses; for example, from Nyabihanga to Rulenge. So the people walk. Just because they are used to it doesn't make it easy, especially when one is carrying thirty or forty pounds of corn or beans on one's head.

Walking has given me a whole new relationship with the people and has resulted in much better communication with them—not only by sharing some of their hardships, but also by meeting them in a personal way—passing them on the road and visiting them in their homes. A missionary priest once told me: "At the beginning in the parish I was prisoner of my 'motor-bike' and keen on speeding. But one fine day I realized that I was traveling twenty-five miles an hour in a community that traveled on foot or on bicycle. So I gave up my motor-bike for the 'bike.' My relations changed immediately. I discovered a new sense of time and distance. I was no longer alone on the road and I took time to stop and visit my friends along the road."

Traveling, whether by car, by bus, or on foot, has often given me an opportunity to learn about myself as well as about other people. When I am late or in a hurry, I can always rationalize why

I can't stop to help a person whose car is stuck on the road. Yet in Africa I've often been aided by people who were willing to give me generously of their time and help. Once, driving a Volkswagen, I suddenly came upon a fork in the muddy road. I took the fork to the right and immediately realized my mistake. My car got stuck in the mud. A few minutes later a bus came by on the correct road. When the driver saw my plight, he stopped the bus and asked eight men to help. Wading into the mud they lifted up my little VW and carried it back to the main road. Another time I was driving near Rulenge in a car packed with luggage and supplies. There was little room for passengers; at most, two people could squeeze in. I came upon three men walking on the side of the road. They signaled for a ride. I stopped. When I explained that there was room for only two people in the car, they politely turned down my offer. They said that they could not leave the third man to walk by himself. So all three continued on foot.

Journey to Nyabihanga

Bishop Christopher and I finally arrived in Rulenge, a small town of several thousand people in northwestern Tanzania, twenty miles from the Burundi border and forty-two miles from the Rwanda border. Its "center" consists mainly of shops, small eating places, government offices, a Catholic hospital, and a hostel. Most of the people live in outlying villages. Rulenge is a division in the government structure and the headquarters of the Rulenge Catholic Diocese. In Shubi, the language of the local Washubi people, Rulenge means "big footprint," and the people immediately think of the track of a lion—a grim reminder of the early history of the area. Even now a lion's roar can be occasionally heard in the middle of the night.

But Rulenge was not my final destination. After three weeks of preparation, on Saturday, September 4, 1976, two Little Brothers of Jesus—Marcel Jagu (French) and Fabian Ntubwa (Zairean)—and I loaded a truck with our belongings and supplies and headed for Nyabihanga, where I was to be stationed.

I rode in the back of the truck with some Tanzanian villagers. It was the end of the long dry season. The first scattered rains had started only the previous week, so the landscape was still bleak and lifeless. At an elevation of 4,600 feet the air was rather cool.

Arriving in Nyabihanga village itself, we passed the village store and grinding machine and the small political-party office with an attached shop that sold salt, sugar, matches, and other commodities. The dirt road wound through the common corn-field of the village to reach "the bishop's house." This title immediately conjured up in my mind a picture of a grand episcopal residence, but this bishop's house was different—a simple mud house with a tin roof, tin doors, and wooden-frame windows. It is called "the bishop's house" because Bishop Christopher Mwoleka himself lives there from time to time.

This mud house was to be my home for the next two years. There was no running water. We fetched water from a spring one-third mile away. There was no electricity. We used kerosene lamps. A filter for drinking water, two tables, several chairs, a bed, a bookshelf, and a cabinet made up the furniture; simple but sufficient. A simple lifestyle would give me an opportunity to share the life of the village people.

As I moved my belongings into the house, I began to think about why I had come to Nyabihanga. I thought about my first journey to Africa, my spiritual pilgrimage around the world, and the slow unfolding of my call-within-a-call. I knew this was all part of a search in the Spirit. Now the search had led me to this spot in Tanzania, to live and share with the people of Nyabihanga village. Here I was in a small village of 140 families, with a total population of 650. I couldn't get more local, more at the grassroots than this.

Our search in this village ministry was for a new style of life, simpler, and closer to the people. Concerning this presence ministry in the villages of Tanzania, Bishop Christopher Mwoleka said, "This is a completely new type of apostolate, which seems to be demanded by our time, and which, to my mind, constitutes a very new call in the church. . . . We seek the being together in community that will make our functioning together for the gospel yield lasting fruits. We are striving for the possibility of pastoral workers who are living a style of life that is truly a witness to the gospel."

As I moved into the bishop's house in Nyabihanga, I looked at the mud walls, the dirt floor, the simple furniture, and as I met the Washubi farmers who came to greet us, I felt like a traveler who had come home. I was ready to live fully the village life, ready to touch basic human experience as I never had before. I knew that I had much to discover and learn from the village people themselves. I was reminded of the words of Henry David Thoreau when he went to live at Walden Pond: "I went to the woods because I wished to live deliberately, to confront only the essential facts of life, and see if I could not learn what it had to teach and not, when I came to die, discover that I had not lived."

Thus I began my life in Nyabihanga, the end of a long search that was a new beginning.

II
Friends and Neighbors

Bishop Christopher Mwoleka enjoys a friendly visit with Scholastica, Sylvia, and our catechist, Astheria Ngenzi (far right). The bishop encouraged the development of lay ministries and a truly local, grassroots church. Many of our best leaders were young women.

In front of my simple mud house with a tin roof in Nyabihanga village, John Monica, Thomas Kidende, and I prepare to leave for the Sunday Eucharist at Bukiriro Outstation. We formed part of the bishop's community and shared the daily life of prayer, cooking, farming and pastoral ministry.

The Christian community gathers for the Sunday Eucharist outside our simple Bukiriro Outstation. This was an opportunity to pray together, talk together and informally share together. Experiencing community is at the heart of the African way of life. Religion and life are one.

The *Ujamaa* Bishop

Two visitors went one day to call on Bishop Christopher Mwoleka, the Catholic bishop of Rulenge Diocese. He was not at his diocesan headquarters in Rulenge town so the visitors were driven to Nyabihanga village, of which the bishop is a member. "As we drove up," the visitors recalled, "we saw a man with some young boys crossing a newly plowed field and coming toward us. The man was barefoot, in dungarees and an old shirt, carrying a pick, sweating, and dirty from his work." It was Bishop Christopher Mwoleka, the man who was responsible for my being in Nyabihanga.

Bishop Mwoleka has been the inspiration and guiding force behind the village ministry in Rulenge Diocese from the very beginning. He was born in Kabondo near Bukoba in 1927. After finishing secondary school he worked as a clerk in a government office in Dar es Salaam for five years before entering the seminary. He was already mature and experienced before studying for the priesthood. After ordination in 1962 he did pastoral work in Buhororo Parish. As a civics teacher at Katoke Minor Seminary he read all of President Julius Nyerere's books and articles on Tanzanian socialism. As he himself says, this reading converted him to *Ujamaa* as a philosophy and as a way of life.

After he became a bishop in 1969, Mwoleka gradually developed his ideas and vision about the role of the church in Tanzanian society, and particularly the role of pastoral workers within the policy of *Ujamaa* and Tanzanian socialism. He has said: "The church and we religious must live and share our lives where the people are. And in Tanzania, the people are in the villages." His plans for a village ministry developed slowly. Over a period of years he arranged for various pastoral workers, especially communities of Sisters, to live in different villages in Rulenge Diocese. The Bernadette Sisters (a local Tanzanian congregation) lived in Nyabihanga village from January 1974 to February 1976. When the Sisters moved, Mwoleka invited the Little Brothers of Jesus to come to Nyabihanga. It was around the time that I felt called to the village ministry, so Bishop Christopher invited me to live in Nyabihanga too.

What kind of man is Mwoleka? He immediately strikes one as a charismatic person, a man of vision who practices what he preaches, who lives what he believes. He stresses that the church should reach out to the people, that pastoral workers should share with the villagers. And he does this himself. He has a room in the bishop's house in Nyabihanga village. From time to time he leaves his office in Rulenge and lives in Nyabihanga. He works in the fields with the villagers, attends the meetings of the village, and participates in the everyday life of Nyabihanga.

Mwoleka is a complex man with many sides. By nature he is quiet and a bit shy. He himself admits that he finds light conversation difficult. Despite this quiet side he is an apostolic extrovert and tries to be a bishop among his people. He has an expressive face. Sometimes he can be stern and very determined-looking, especially when emphasizing a point he believes in. At other times he breaks into a hearty laugh. Being a deeply prayerful man, his mood is often one of serious introspection, but when a visitor arrives he is always the cheerful host and attentive listener. With these different sides to his character, we laughingly refer to Christopher No. 1 and Christopher No. 2.

Bishop Christopher always strikes one as a man of integrity. When he speaks, his warm, deep-set eyes are sincere. When he becomes enthusiastic about something, he can be spellbinding, as when he talks about the village ministry: "The government is busy making the structures for our villages, but the villages will be soulless if they are not oriented by God. Our job is to put the soul into the village."

The bishop's overriding concern is to break the traditional dualism of life—body and spirit, secular and religious. He says, "The life of a Christian shouldn't be divided any more in two parts, that is, a time of serving 'mammon' and a time of serving God. By harmonizing spiritual and material life, Christians are able to serve the One Lord God, always and everywhere. We therefore want *to live a way of life that will satisfy our material and spiritual needs at the same time.* . . . Now the time has come for Christians to unify their lives; to serve God by earning a living and to earn a living by serving God." At another time he wrote about the

> search for viable pastoral structures and style of life which could help in this work of re-educating ourselves in order that we may be truly salt of the earth. We have to learn to be a community of God by integrating ourselves into the existing communities of men and women as they are now in our day. . . . We believe we are responding to the call of the Holy Spirit who is at work in this new age in order to integrate the material with the spiritual, the secular with the religious, the active with the contemplative, the individual with the community. Our response, therefore, has got to be guided by this Holy Spirit to whom we have to be in tune through prayer, sacrifice, and discernment.

Bishop Christopher feels that *Ujamaa* and Tanzanian socialism offer a great opportunity for the church to witness to these gospel values in society.

During my six years with AMECEA in Nairobi I worked with many bishops of Eastern Africa. A good number are considered traditional, if not conservative, "Roman African bishops rather than African bishops," as one person put it. But Bishop Mwoleka is different. I have often asked myself why. It is not that he is a liberal or a revolutionary. In fact, he is a blend of the old and the new. When he is convinced about traditional pastoral practices, he firmly resists change in the church. He is opposed to ordaining catechists or women, to revising the church ban on polygamy, to introducing certain ways of Africanizing the liturgy. He is different in that he is a searcher who is not afraid to experiment and try new things. He struggles to find the truth, to be authentic, to live the gospel values in Tanzania today. In addition to the village ministry, he has pioneered in such new ideas as integrated, or mixed, communities (priests, Brothers, Sisters, laymen and laywomen living together and working together in pastoral teams); the Seven-Year Leadership Training Program to develop SCCs; Sisters running parishes and outstations; minor-seminary training that integrates study, manual work, and sharing in the ordinary life of the villagers.

As a searcher Mwoleka is constantly developing and refining his ideas. He will eloquently explain his position on certain issues, but if better ideas are presented he is not afraid to change his mind. Since he regularly revises and updates his views and plans, he at times appears to be inconsistent or unclear to those who are not familiar with his searching style. As a result, some African priests in Rulenge Diocese have not understood the bishop's vision about pastoral workers living in villages or the importance of developing SCCs.

It was Bishop Christopher Mwoleka the searcher who drew me to Nyabihanga village to continue my own search.

"My Friend the Lapsed Pagan"

One of our closest neighbors was Nchabukoroka (which means, in Shubi, "the fruit that has fallen"). He was the elected leader or headman of our ten-family grouping or cell. This grouping is the official unit of Tanzanian people on the local level in each village. Nchabukoroka, as our neighborhood leader, was responsible for coordinating our common work in the village fields.

"Officially" Nchabukoroka was a member of an African traditional religion (which formerly we distainfully called "pagan" religion). He had two wives, Aurelia and Adriana, both baptized Christians. Aurelia had had five children, three of whom were living: Patricia, aged fifteen; Mattias, aged five; and Chiza, nine months. Nchabukoroka prayed and used the sign of the cross. He occasionally attended the Eucharist service and the weekly Bible service of Nyabuliga SCC. From time to time he worked on the farm plot of our SCC. I called him "my friend the lapsed pagan."

My experience has convinced me that there are no nonbelievers in East Africa. The African people have a deep religious sense and an awareness of the presence of God in their lives. Even though their religious beliefs may not fit into Western categories of institutional religions, the people certainly are not pagans. To Africans such as Nchabukoroka, God, the Supreme Being, is meaningful and very real.

Reflecting on the deep spirituality of African traditional religions, I was led to rethink many Western distinctions and categories. Statistically, Nyabihanga village was about 30 percent Catholic and 70 percent non-Catholic. But what did this really mean? We hardly ever distinguished between "Catholic" and "Protestants." There were only a few Protestants in the village, so everyone who was baptized was called a Christian (= Catholic). But many were Christian in name only, such as those persons who had been baptized as infants in danger of death, but who had never practiced the Christian faith later. Some members of the African traditional religions were more active in the SCCs than the Christians themselves.

Nchabukoroka and I had a friendship that went beyond distinctions and categories. He was thirty-nine years old and I was forty, just a year apart. When I first arrived in Nyabihanga he taught me to use a hoe in the Washubi way. For selfish reasons I enjoyed cultivating or weeding next to Nchabukoroka in the common fields. He was very strong and did the work of two men, so he helped me when I fell behind.

Of medium height, Nchabukoroka was slender and wiry. He was very agile, and I'm sure he would have been a soccer star if he had had the chance. By nature the Washubi people are reserved, but Nchabukoroka always had a ready smile and an animated conversational style. His excitement about life helped him to be a natural leader. During the 1977 election for a new chairperson of Nyabihanga village he came in second. He was a member of the village council and in charge of the Nyabihanga village bar (a very popular job!).

The Short Lives
of Emmanuel and John

Thursday, December 23: Aurelia, Nchabukoroka's first wife, gave birth to twin boys. There was great rejoicing in our neighborhood.

Friday, December 24: Since I was in Rulenge, Nchabukoroka called the elderly catechist Salvatori Bahuwimbuye to baptize the twins. The local church custom was to baptize twins immediately, since many of them died soon after birth. For the local people this Christian tradition was combined with the African traditional religion custom of having a "naming ceremony." Among the Washubi the birth of twins was a sign of bad fortune, but giving babies names could protect them from the evil spirits. Because it was near the Christmas season, the two boys were given the names Emmanuel and John.

Saturday, December 25: The rejoicing and celebrating at the twins' birth continued. Many people came to see the babies. Friends and neighbors brought gifts. The women helped Aurelia by fetching water and firewood. In my Christmas homily I commented on the close parallel between the birth of Jesus Christ and the birth of twins for the Washubi people. I stressed the meaning of the name Emmanuel: "God is with us."

Sunday, December 26: The celebrating (and drinking) continued.

Monday, December 27: Feast of Saint John the Apostle. The second-born twin, John, died late in the evening—on his feast day.

Tuesday, December 28: John was buried in the morning in the banana plantation behind Nchabukoroka's hut. In the Washubi tradition burial usually takes place within a day after a person dies. The men took turns digging the grave. The women sat at a distance wailing. Young people were not allowed to attend the burial of a twin. A tall, stately man from Bukiriro village named Bikeba conducted the burial ceremony. He officiated at all burials of twins. With his gaunt frame, white beard, and rhythmic stride, he made one think of a prophet. He first painted the walls of the grave with a dark mud, a special Washubi custom to appease and ward off the evil spirits afterward. The baby was wrapped in a reed mat of the kind the people sleep on in their homes. As the people sleep in life, so they sleep after death.

That afternoon I celebrated the Eucharist for the "repose of John's soul." It was the Feast of the Holy Innocents. About thirty people, including Nchabukoroka, attended the liturgy.

Late that same evening Emmanuel died.

Wednesday, December 29: Emmanuel was buried in the morning. After the evening Eucharist I blessed the two graves with holy water.

Death comes suddenly in Africa, especially to children. The twins probably died of pneumonia, since they were not sufficiently protected from the night cold. Many mothers lay their babies near the warmth of a wood fire. But at night the fires go down and the babies easily catch cold.

The local church custom of baptizing twins immediately, even if the parents belong to an African traditional religion or are non-practicing Catholics, posed a real pastoral dilemma for me. Theologically I had great reservations about this practice. I felt it perpetuated a quantitative rather than a qualitative Christianity. Often there was no assurance that the parents would bring up the child in the Catholic faith. Many times they just wanted the power of the Christian naming ceremony to ward off the evil spirits. I felt that going along with this "numbers game" would be an obstacle both to the growth of a deeply rooted Christianity and to the possibility of an ongoing Christian formation.

Gradually we changed the pastoral approach in Bukiriro outstation. For the baptism of twins (and all other children as well), we explained, at least one parent must be a practicing Catholic who is willing to watch over the Christian upbringing of the child or children. Otherwise, there would be no baptism, and later (after entering the fourth grade) the child could choose to be baptized or not. In addition, parents and godparents must attend prebaptism instructions to learn more about the meaning of the sacrament and their own responsibilities. In various instructions and homilies we emphasized the meaning of baptism in relation to the SCC to which the child, parents, and godparents belonged.

I discovered that this process of religious education demands much time. But gradually the Christian leaders and some of the parents themselves took more responsibility in examining the parents and godparents and preparing them for the baptism of their children. Explanations were given especially during the weekly Bible service of the SCCs.

On one occasion, when the bishop was staying with us in Nyabihanga, Katarataro, one of our neighbors who belonged to an African traditional religion, asked for baptism for his newborn twins. Clearly he wanted the "power" of Christian names to protect his children from the evil spirits. In refusing him, the bishop shrewdly drew a comparison with African family traditions.

Parents, he said, always make sure to sample the food before giving it to their children. Comparing the Christian life to food, Bishop Mwoleka asked Katarataro: "Would you give food to your children that you won't eat yourself?" The meaning was clear: How could Katarataro ask for baptism for his children when he did not want to be baptized himself? Katarataro had no answer to the bishop's question. He walked away, sad but with plenty to think about.

The people in Nyabihanga have a patient resignation, almost a fatalism, about death. For them it is inevitable. In almost every family at least one child had died. As they do in so many events, Africans attribute death to God, the highest cause, saying: "It is by God's action that he died." To reason with them about the actual cause of death, or the importance of getting medicine early, or having a balanced diet is difficult.

When a child is very sick there is a certain quiet, almost a hush, in the neighborhood, like the calm before a heavy rainstorm. When I hear the crying and wailing of the women I know that death has come. When a member of an African traditional religion dies, as Nabuzoya, the granddaughter of our neighbor Mzee Paulo, did, the Little Brothers and I go to sit with the other men outside the house. There is little else to do. But the very sitting is a sharing in the grief of the family and an important sign. Westerners would want to do something more than just sitting with bereaved people, but this is not the African way.

After someone dies there is a custom for two men to sleep at the house of the deceased for three consecutive nights—different men each night. This is a way of sharing the grief and sadness of the family. The two men talk with the father of the family until late into the night to keep his mind off his sadness and despair.

Likewise, when a neighbor or a member of the clan dies, the Washubi custom is not to use a hoe (the basic symbol of manual work in the fields) for three days. This is a sign of the mourning period and of respect for the deceased person. One is permitted to do small jobs around one's house, but not to work on one's farm with a hoe.

I have often wondered how this reverence for death and the mourning period might fit into our task-oriented Western societies, where the work ethic is so important and every working minute precious. Even in Nyabihanga, when I put aside my hoe for three days, I sometimes felt uneasy about all the work that wouldn't get done. Now I have come to feel that when Africans put aside their hoes for three days, they not only teach us about the meaning of death, but about the meaning of life as well.

When someone dies, time is not important. Often friends and relatives arrive after the burial. This can happen for one of several reasons: slow communications, poor transportation facilities, or the custom of having the burial soon after death in tropical Africa where preserving the body is difficult. Africans who arrive after the funeral show their respect and reverence for the deceased person by their presence, and by sharing in the grief of the bereaved family. Often they bring food for the mourners and stay for a few days to help the bereaved family with the cooking and various chores around the house. Depending on the customs of varying peoples, the mourning period can last for weeks, with prescribed rites taking place at fixed periods.

These African traditions are very different from funeral customs in the United States. Americans make a real effort to attend the funeral itself, but the focus is on the ceremony, the official function. If a person cannot come for the funeral (bad weather, impossible airline connections, other pressing business), he or she will telephone the bereaved family, and all concerned will usually understand. But to come a few days after the funeral is quite rare. There is a difference also between sending flowers (which can be an automatic gesture) and personally bringing flowers or some other gift. The person-centeredness of African funerals and the mourning period have much to teach Westerners.

I have also discovered that Africans are not afraid of death, perhaps because they live so close to death all the time. In an African's cosmic view death is not traumatic; at death a person joins the ancestral community. I remember once talking with the catechist Salvatori about death. He told me, "I am not afraid of death, but I am afraid of hunger." At first I did not understand what he meant. He then explained that he was not afraid of death because it is an ordinary thing, a "thing of the world." Sooner or later it comes to everyone. No one can escape death. But hunger was different—uncertain and unpredictable. Hunger is very hard to control and makes a person helpless. It also produces a deep fear of the unknown.

Another villager explained it to me this way. Basic to the African worldview is the idea of *utu*, which means "personality" or "personhood." The act of dying itself is not losing one's personhood, but dying of hunger is to lose one's personhood. Dying of hunger makes a person less than human. It has the same result as slavery, inequality, or oppression.

Gaudensia's First Ride

One week we attended a seminar in Rulenge on building SCCs. Among the participants from Nyabihanga were two young girls, Gaudensia and Aurelia. They were about eighteen years old, having recently finished the seventh grade, the last year of primary school in Tanzania. To attend the seminar they walked the eleven miles from Nyabihanga to Rulenge. Even though they had lived in Nyabihanga all their lives, it was their first trip to Rulenge.

To go from a village of 650 people to a town of several thousand people was a big event, a momentous undertaking for the two girls, almost comparable to the astronauts' trip to the moon. Everything was new, different, exciting, mysterious.

This event helped me to realize that you can't take things for granted or assume that everyone's experience is the same. For Gaudensia eleven miles was a big distance. For people living in Rulenge to take the bus to Mwanza (a distance of 235 miles) was a big adventure. Yet people living in Mwanza might think nothing of such a bus ride. For them to make the 735-mile trip to Dar es Salaam was a new and exciting adventure. It all depends on one's background and experience. A Swahili proverb puts it very well: "The water in a coconut shell is like an ocean to an ant."

After the seminar, crowded together in an open truck, we all returned to Nyabihanga. Just before we set off, Gaudensia became very frightened. She had never ridden in any kind of car or vehicle before. The truck was so high off the ground. The back was open to the wind and dust. She was scared of the truck's speed. So she asked if she could sit between the driver and another passenger inside the cab. She felt safer there.

A Visitor from Nairobi

After living in Nyabihanga for about six weeks, I received my first overnight visitor—Father Joseph Mukwaya, the Ugandan priest who had succeeded me as the social communications secretary of AMECEA. He had come to Rulenge to attend a communications workshop and took the occasion to visit me.

Joe is one of my closest friends. During the one day we spent together in Nyabihanga we reminisced about our many experiences together, and he told me about the progress of the Social Communications Office in Nairobi. He felt at home with my neighbors, and took part in the common work of our ten-family cell.

In the afternoon we visited some of the neighbors, who had expected that I would bring Joe to see them, as they were eager to welcome my friend. When a visitor comes, members of the family drop everything to welcome the guest. A meal is prepared, and everyone sits around the table for hours exchanging news and experiences. There is no concern about the passage of time.

I have seen this tradition of dropping everything to welcome a visitor repeated again and again in Nyabihanga village. The welcome is always spontaneous and generous. Joe Mukwaya had often demonstrated this to me while I was working with him in Nairobi. Whenever an unexpected visitor came, he would drop everything, welcome the guest, show the person around, and talk eagerly. I always found this difficult. Even though I promised ahead of time to give myself completely to the next visitor, when the moment came I would be conscious of the passing of time and the neglect of my work.

The uniqueness of African hospitality has been manifested to me not only in our little village, but in all of Tanzania and in other African countries. The traditions of hospitality are deep and sincere, and reveal themselves in many ways. When you approach a house, the first thing the householder will say is "Karibu," which means "Welcome." Often a person will say, "I welcome you with both hands held out in friendship."

Different peoples have different customs of hospitality, but my experiences with the Wasukuma, the largest ethnic group in Tanzania, seem very special. Once, after I had stayed five days in a village in Tanzania, the Wasukuma Christians insisted on preparing a farewell meal for me. In fact, each family wished to prepare its own meal to say goodbye. The result was that on that day I started eating lunch at 10:30 A.M. and finished the fifth lunch at 1:00 P.M. With a very full stomach I prepared to leave. Even then the wife of one of the Christians came running up to say, "But you haven't eaten our food yet."

Together with this rare hospitality the Wasukuma have a deep sense of gratitude. A Sukuma cathechist from Shinyanga Diocese once visited me for five days to learn about building SCCs. After returning home he wrote: "I would like to offer thanks for all that you did for me from the first minute of living together with you to the exchanging of the handshake of goodbye."

But within these traditions of hospitality the visitor has certain responsibilities. A guest who stays for some time is expected to take part in the work of the family. A Swahili proverb says: "A visitor is a guest for two days; on the third day give the person a hoe."

African hospitality is basically person-centered. In our community in Nyabihanga we took turns cooking. Often we would spend some minutes in chapel before the meal. So when the table was set, and the food ready, the cook for that particular day would say: "Karibu chakula" ("Welcome to the food"). This invitation always sounded so much better to me than "Chakula tayari" (Swahili for "The food is ready").

For Africans, eating is a social event. The focus is on human relationships and sharing together, rather than merely eating to get strength and energy. Feasts are a group experience that emphasize the importance of the extended family.

The spontaneous hospitality of the Africans seems to have a deep Christian meaning. To be available to others, to get out of oneself and one's own needs, and to enter into the life and experience of another person is to be what Christ has so aptly been described as: "A man for others." In the homilies, sermons, and talks in Rulenge Diocese we often referred to *ubinafsi*, which means "individualism" or "selfishness." It is just the opposite of the Tanzanian values of *Ujamaa* ("Familyhood") and *jumuiya* ("community"). A deep and sincere sense of hospitality can break down *ubinafsi* and the selfish concern for one's personal needs and plans.

The visit of Joe Mukwaya to Nyabihanga reminded me of the great gift I have received through having very close African friends. When I first came to Africa, an older missionary priest told me, "You will really begin to understand the African people and culture when you can honestly say, 'My closest friends are Africans—closer than the priests and Brothers in my missionary society, closer than my other friends and co-workers.' " Now I can joyfully and gratefully say that my closest friends in Africa are Africans; friends such as Father Joe Mukwaya, Bishop Christopher Mwoleka, Sister Mary Nives Kizito (a Ugandan Sister), and others. These friends have helped me to discover and love Africa and Africans "from the inside." I have received much more than I have given. But mainly we have shared. And in sharing with these friends I have experienced the meaning of the Christian life in many ways. I thank God our Father for the rich grace and blessing of these friendships.

Yet I am aware of certain limitations in these friendships, due especially to our cross-cultural situation. Even though we speak in Swahili, I realize that I can't talk to Joe Mukwaya and Sister Mary Nives in their own family language, Luganda. Nor can I talk with Bishop Mwoleka in his own family language, Haya. I will always be somewhat of an outsider to their families and clans, their national customs and traditions. Then there are parts of my own American heritage and traditions that I can't fully share with them. I find it especially hard to explain the meaning of my missionary vocation—why I left family, friends, home, and country to live in Africa.

But beyond and beneath these limitations and other differences is something deeper and more important—the love and friendship we share together. Most important is what we share together in Christ. We are brothers and sisters together in the family of God, in the Christian community.

Our Bukiriro Community

The two villages of Nyabihanga and Bukiriro form the outstation of Bukiriro, where I celebrated the Eucharist every Sunday for the local Christian community. *Bukiriro* means "the place of being saved," an appropriate name for the site of a church, God's house. Not that salvation is linked to a place, a building. Salvation is a gift from God, an affair of the heart. But the Bukiriro church, God's house, is a source, a spring, a fountain of God's saving grace; it is the sign of the local faith-community praying, sharing, and witnessing together, celebrating God's presence among us, hearing the Word of God, the Good News of salvation, receiving Christ in the Eucharist, going forth to be a sign and leaven in the larger community.

My two years of walking to Bukiriro to celebrate the Sunday liturgy with two hundred to three hundred Christians left many impressions: greeting the Christians on the narrow path on a glistening Sunday morning; joining the Christians early on Palm Sunday to cut fresh palm branches for use in the procession; watching the laughing schoolchildren in their bright blue-and-yellow uniforms washing at the river before walking up the hill to the church; experiencing the sudden silence on entering the simple mud-brick church with its tin roof and dirt floor; watching the flickering kerosene lamp at the midnight Eucharist on Easter and Christmas while the joyful shouts of "Alleluia" and "Happy Feast Day" rang out.

I would reach Bukiriro early Sunday morning after a half-hour walk from Nyabihanga. Many schoolchildren would have already arrived for Sunday school, a preparation to receive baptism, first Communion, and confirmation. I would have plenty of time to talk and share with the Christians before and after the Eucharist; to greet the elders in the few words of Shubi that I knew; to joke with the children; to discuss plans for the church farm or a future seminar with the lay leaders.

It was a real joy to be able to celebrate the Eucharist for the same Christian community every Sunday. After the liturgy I didn't have to rush off to another outstation. I could "be with" the Christians rather than "do for them" and then leave. So gradually I became part of the Bukiriro Christian community. The Christians were my Bukiriro family. In Nyabihanga Christians were few (and the serious ones even fewer). But there were many Christians in Bukiriro: faithful women who never missed the Sunday Eucharist; a large and active group of young boys and girls, especially those in the church choir; and zealous leaders on the outstation council. These Christians were the heart of Bukiriro outstation.

I was wholeheartedly adopted into the Bukiriro Christian community. Salvatori Bahuwimbuye, the old, retired catechist, started working as catechist before I was born. He called himself the first twin. Petro Gwanka, the faithful chairperson of the outstation council, was the second twin. And they called me the third twin. While this did not make sense logically, the real sense was the heart sense. I really felt at home with the Bukiriro Christians, part of them, one with them. I often visited them in their homes. We talked together, worked on the church farm together, and occasionally ate together.

By being closely identified with one outstation and one Christian community, I had the opportunity to experiment with various new pastoral approaches. We strove for a qualitative rather than a quantitative Christianity, a real deepening of the Christian faith and Christian living. The key was daily contact with the people.

Bukiriro was one of the twenty-one outstations of Rulenge Parish. The parish priest was Father Lazaro Kadende, whose own home was about forty miles from Bukiriro. He spoke Shubi perfectly and knew the customs and traditions of the local people much better than I did. Yet Lazaro said that I had one advantage that he didn't have—daily contact with the people. Together with the assistant parish priest, Lazaro was responsible for twenty outstations. I was responsible for one—Bukiriro. The daily contact with the Christian community of Bukiriro outstation and the village communities of Bukiriro and Nyabihanga gave me insights into the daily lives of the people. I met them and shared with them in their homes, in the fields, on the road. I knew almost everyone by name—even though I found many of the Washubi names hard to pronounce. Through this daily contact I related more easily to the ordinary life of the people, their problems, their concerns, their hopes. By actually living in one of the two villages of the outstation, identification and sharing with the people were much easier.

Bishop Christopher Mwoleka and others hope and plan that more and more priests and other pastoral workers will be able to live and work away from the parish center—more on the local level such as the subparish, the outstation, the village. Even if a priest is responsible for a section of the parish (for example, a group of five outstations) he could cover this section from a village or outstation, not from the parish center itself. President Julius Nyerere understood this very well, as he showed when he said, "The main thing is that he [priest, missionary] lives in one village and is identified with the life of that village, even if his work takes him to many other areas."

In Tanzania the thrust has begun toward a "village" (*kijiji*) church. Pastoral work focuses on where the Christians are actually living, not on an administrative structure where the parish headquarters is the center of everything. This marks a decisive policy of decentralization and localization. Gradually more responsibility is being given to lay people. They are the leaders and animators of the church on the local level, especially in the outstations and the villages.

This new pastoral emphasis on the villages where most of the Tanzanian people actually live is closely linked to the great stress on the development of SCCs. An SCC is a caring, sharing, faith-reflecting, praying, and serving community in which ongoing Christian formation takes place. It may consist of an existing community, a neighborhood grouping of five to fifteen families, people with common interests or activities, and so on. It is a natural community or grouping based on geographical proximity, blood relationship, occupation, social ties, and other affinities. It is the basic place of evangelization and catechesis. The new pastoral aim is to base church life on these SCCs. Bishop Mwoleka once said that in Rulenge Diocese "the entire pastoral work will be carried out by means of small Christian communities." This is no vague dream, but a dramatic shift in pastoral planning supported by a detailed seven-year plan for training leaders (especially lay leaders) to animate the SCCs.

The priority given to the village church and SCCs in Tanzania is the result of serious thinking, planning, and pastoral practice in the church in Eastern Africa. A brief look at recent developments follow.

1. At the AMECEA Study Conference in December 1973 the Catholic bishops of Eastern Africa (Kenya, Malawi, Tanzania, Uganda, and Zambia) stated:

> We are convinced that in these countries of Eastern Africa it is time for the church to become really "local," that is: self-ministering, self-propagating, and self-supporting. Our planning is aimed at building up such local churches for the coming years. We believe that in order to achieve this we have to insist on building church life and work on basic Christian communities in both rural and urban areas. Church life must be based on the communities in which everyday life and work take place: those basic and manageable social groupings whose members can experience real interpersonal relationships and feel a sense of communal belonging, both in living and in work. We believe that Christian communities at this level will be best suited to develop intense vitality and to become effective witnesses in their natural environment.

2. The AMECEA Study Conference in July 1976 stated:

> Systematic formation of small Christian communities should be the key pastoral priority in the years to come within Eastern Africa. . . . The task of building Christian communities is more one of creating and developing awareness of what our renewed vision of the church means in practical terms and relationships than one of building new structures. This can be achieved by study and dialogue, by the giving of responsibilities to the communities and by encouraging local initiatives. This principle of localization involves a change of attitude and mentality on the part of both church authorities and of the Catholic people as a whole.

3. Bishop Patrick Kalilombe of Malawi has pointed out that these statements of the bishops mark:

> a decisive landmark in our pastoral policy in Eastern Africa. For the bishops, the resolve to base Christian life and witness on small Christian communities is not just one way among many possible ones; it is not just following a passing fad in the church today. It is a basic commitment; a serious shift in pastoral emphasis. It is deliberately intended to modify deeply our pastoral system, policy, and practice. Until now the avowed common system was to base the life of the church on the parish level, rather than on the subparish level. . . .
>
> In these circumstances of Eastern Africa, what we call missions or parishes cannot be taken as the basic units of the local church. If so, the church is doomed to failure. We need to adopt a new system whereby the basic units of the church are those smaller communities where the ordinary life of the people takes place. If we want the church to live and function actually as a community, then we must go down to that smaller level at which people live and interact in their daily life. It is in these smaller communities that the church can express itself in a meaningful Christian communion. Such a basic community would be the only realistic base for the church's existence and effectiveness. Here is where the church can exist as an authentic communion. The wider dimensions of the church are not one community, but a communion of communities. The parish is a communion of basic communities within the parish area.

In some ways this is a revolutionary pastoral plan that makes the local church a reality, and makes lay people truly responsible for their church. The emphasis is on a grassroots church, where there is a bottom-up rather than a top-down approach.

Putting this plan into action dramatically changed Bukiriro outstation. In November 1976 fourteen SCCs were started, nine in Bukiriro village and five in Nyabihanga village. Each SCC was a grouping of families living near each other (a neighborhood group). We followed the ten-family cell plan that the Tanzanian government uses to group people together in the villages. So Bukiriro outstation became a "community of communities," a "communion of communities." Each SCC elected its own representative to the Bukiriro outstation council. So each basic community, each natural grouping of Christians on the local level, had a voice in the planning and decision-making of the whole outstation. The Christians thus felt more responsible for their church.

Shifting the responsibility to the laity was not easy. In fact it was a long and arduous process. In the area of Bukiriro outstation, as in many places in the world, there was a long tradition of "the priest will do it" and "let the parish handle it." The Christians remained largely passive, and, as Salvatori told me, "We are used to receiving everything." The priest was the church, and the faithful were mere beneficiaries.

Two experiences dramatized this situation for me: (1) I went to one area where a survey of the local Christians was being taken. They were given a series of statements starting with "The church says . . . ." When asked who "the church" referred to, over 90 percent said "church" referred to bishops. They thought any statement by the church came from the bishops, who made all the decisions. (2) In seminars I often posed this question: "If a visitor came to your town or village and asked you: 'Where is the church?' what would you answer?" Over 95 percent answered that they would take the visitor to the physical church building. When I pointed out that the Christians, the faithful themselves, are the church, the people were amazed. Only later did they say, "We should have told that visitor: 'We are the church.' "

In my own ministry I often felt that I was merely dispensing the sacraments, that I was a clerical attendant running an ecclesiastical service station. The Christians would come in, fill up their sacramental tanks, and then go off. An even deeper problem was that this service was limited to small segments of the lives of the Christians, mostly on Sunday mornings. Ongoing Christian formation was very difficult.

But in Bukiriro outstation I discovered new possibilities. First, the local Christians were open and willing. They were ready to respond; they just needed someone to help them get started. Second, daily contact with the local Christian community provided many opportunities for a deeper, more integrated Christianity. Third, the pastoral plan of the SCCs provided a unique way to integrate religion into the everyday life and work of the people.

The process itself was slow, but over a period of two years we had many encouraging results. Gradually the Christians realized that I was not going to make the decisions. My role was to be an animator. After about six months, Nicodemus Kacharuzi, the chairperson of the Rulenge Parish Council, visited us for five days and conducted a seminar for the outstation leaders. At the end of his visit I asked him for an evaluation of the outstation and especially of my own pastoral work. He mentioned that the Christians were confused when I would only suggest something. The laity were used to the priest deciding (just as the villagers were used to the chairperson of the village deciding). The Christians were used to following the laws and decisions of the church. To hear suggestions and possibilities (even the possibility that they could decide questions such as the use of church money or how to expand the church building) was new. But Nicodemus strongly encouraged me to continue. He clearly saw that it was the way of the future, especially if the laity—more than 99 percent of the church—were going to assume their rightful responsibilities. It took another year before the lay leaders of Bukiriro outstation began to assume more responsibilities themselves.

The SCCs were an especially good training ground for leaders. Laymen and laywomen received training and experience in conducting the weekly Bible services, reading the Bible, leading the songs, teaching religion to the children, administering the money of the SCCs, and carrying out other pastoral activities. The young people responded most enthusiastically. If they had not actually conducted a meeting, taught a religion class, or read the Bible aloud, they would not have taken responsibility for the affairs of their own outstation, their own church. "The whole community" is a basic idea in traditional African society. The Christians at Bukiriro thus started to understand the importance of "catechesis by the whole community for the whole community."

After two years of this new approach there were signs of new life. The Christians were still slow in taking the initiative themselves; there was still a lack of creative thinking; but there were signs of progress in the people's self-reliance, in a sharp rise in vocations, and in their reaching out to help other outstations. These signs designate a truly local church: self-supporting, self-ministering, and self-propagating.

In some dioceses of Tanzania (for example, Mwanza Diocese), self-reliance has been a reality for a long time. But in parts of Rulenge Diocese, especially the parishes near Rulenge town itself, self-reliance is a new concept. After one year of experimentation the lay leaders started to administer the funds of Bukiriro outstation. The result was that the amount of the Sunday collection, the yearly church tax, and various special collections tripled. There were three reasons for this. First, the leaders of the outstation regularly explained the use of the money that was collected. Second, the treasurer and other leaders visited the Christians on a regular basis to explain the importance of self-reliance and the various ways to achieve it, such as maintaining the church farm, selling trees on the church property, renting the house on the church property, contributing part of the bean harvest to the church fund, and so forth. Third, the structure of the SCCs made it convenient for each SCC to start its own community farm plot and community treasury.

Up to 1977 no local priests, Brothers, or Sisters had gone out from Bukiriro outstation. The few who entered the seminary or the religious life left after a short time. But in 1978, owing largely to the dynamic life of the SCCs, there was a vocation explosion. One young man entered the minor seminary. Another entered the Franciscan Brothers. One young woman entered the Bernadette Sisters (the local diocesan congregation), and four more applied to enter the following year. Two young men and a young woman entered a special "Integrated Community" started by Bishop Mwoleka in which priests, Sisters, laymen, and laywomen live and work together. All these young people were leaders in their respective SCCs.

After the SCCs had been firmly established in Bukiriro outstation, the lay leaders began helping neighboring outstations. They visited Rwinyana, Bugarama, and Kihinga outstations to encourage the prayer leaders and religious-formation leaders of the SCCs in these areas. They helped out during a Small Christian Community Seminar at Rurama outstation. This "outreach" helped the Bukiriro Christians not only to deepen their own commitment and zeal, but to understand that "the whole church is missionary," and that they have a responsibility to spread the faith to other communities.

Another sign of the growing maturity of the Christians of Bukiriro was their ecumenical spirit. Distinctions among different Christian denominations disappeared. Everyone was welcome to attend the weekly Bible service of the SCCs—Catholics, Protestants, members of African traditional religions. Everyone was welcome to participate in the Sunday liturgy and recollection days. While the lay leaders carefully checked on who was permitted to receive the sacraments, the overall emphasis was on the whole community praying together.

This ecumenical spirit was shown once when the members of the Bukiriro outstations council met to decide who would be allowed to rent the house that had been vacated by the retired religion teacher. Three men applied: two Catholics and one Protestant, who usually prayed at the Anglican church four miles away. After carefully examining the personal character and family life of the three men, the council members chose the Protestant man because they felt he gave the best Christian example.

In speaking of ecumenism an Indian archbishop lamented that the divisions of Christianity in Europe were brought to Africa and Asia by missionaries and others. He stated that it would have been much better if these divisions had remained in Europe, for they were Europe's problem. The traditional values of the people of Africa and Asia are unity and community, and it was tragic that the historical divisions of Christianity now divided the people of these continents. So it was encouraging to see that these historical divisions of Christianity did not affect the unity of the Christians in places like Bukiriro.

Mzee Patrice

Several times each year Mzee ("Elder" or "Old Man") Patrice, a relative of Bishop Mwoleka, came from Bukoba to Nyabihanga to help us in our banana plantation, because he was a specialist in cultivating our many varieties of bananas.

About five feet, six inches tall, Patrice was thin and wiry. With his short-cropped gray hair and wrinkled face, he sometimes wore a stern expression. At other times his hearty laugh revealed many missing teeth. His big, callused hands spoke of many years of cultivating banana trees. Villagers in Nyabihanga called him "the young man," which always brought a roar of laughter from his deep chest. He loved cigarettes and no arguments about the dangers of smoking could ever convince him to change.

From the time Mzee Patrice and I began living together I tried to get to know him, to understand him, and to share with him. Many people would have said that a foreigner could never get to know an African such as Patrice. They would have pointed out the many differences between us. Patrice was over seventy years old; I didn't know his first language, Haya, and he didn't know English. He had lived in the West Lake region of Tanzania all his life. Our backgrounds, education, and interests were vastly different. Yet we had one very important thing in common. We had both come to Nyabihanga to live with the local people. So I tried hard to get to know, understand, and love Patrice.

As I struggled with this, I was reminded of some advice I had read more than fifteen years ago in Harper Lee's *To Kill a Mockingbird*: "You never really understand a person until you consider things from his point of view, until you climb into his skin and walk around in it."

I decided that if I really wanted to understand Patrice I had to get inside him to see the way he saw, to feel the way he felt. I knew that many missionaries believed this to be impossible; a foreigner could never think and feel like an African. I recalled a conversation with a Canadian White Father who had spent many years in Uganda. He knew the Baganda people and their language and customs well, yet he realized that for the foreigner, for the missionary from another country and culture, the African will always remain a mystery. Once he said to me, "I would give twenty years of my life for a thirty-second bicycle ride through the mind of an African." I must admit that Patrice always remained somewhat of a mystery to me, but we had some interesting experiences together, and these experiences helped me to glimpse the African character and African way of life.

With his sheer dedication and perseverance Mzee Patrice

taught me a great deal. Although adult education was stressed by the Tanzanian government, few adults in Nyabihanga actually learned to read and write. They attended classes three times a week out of duty rather than conviction. But Patrice was different. In the late afternoons I would come to his small room to find him practicing his reading. Sitting on the edge of his bed he would slowly and laboriously read out loud. His wrinkled index finger would trace each line as he pronounced one word at a time. Occasionally he would ask me for pamphlets on the church. He was deeply religious and enjoyed reading about the Christian faith.

My friendship with Patrice challenged me to reflect deeply on evangelical poverty and simplicity. Patrice was truly a simple man, and I was touched, when I helped him to unpack, to see how few were his material goods: two blankets, two pairs of short pants, a flashlight, a rosary, a machete, and a moon-shaped knife to cut banana stalks.

All Washubi farmers live simply. Compared with people of Western countries, and even those of the more developed parts of Tanzania, they are very poor. Food is scarce. Early in the morning the people go to the fields on an empty stomach. The first meal is around 1 P.M.—the staple diet of beans and bananas. A similar meal is served in the evening. This is not a balanced diet, and the bloated stomachs and thin arms and legs of the small children show that they suffer from extreme malnutrition.

Many little children run around naked, and many adults have only one set of clothes. I recall one Sunday when we celebrated the baptismal anniversary of the dauthter of one of our lay leaders in Bukiriro outstation. The girl's mother failed to come to the Eucharist. The day before, she had washed the African cloth that the women use as part of their dress and a sudden shower on Saturday afternoon had caused her clothes to be still damp on Sunday morning.

On another occasion on short notice we were invited to send three Christians to a lay-leadership seminar in Rulenge. They ought to have begun their journey the very next day, but as Salvatori gently reminded me, "Our delegates have only one set of clothes; they have to wash them before they go to Rulenge. So maybe they won't be ready to go tomorrow."

But lack of food, lack of a balanced diet, or lack of clothes wasn't what struck me the most. What affected me most strongly was the way the Washubi had to live at the survival level so much of the time. With frequent sickness, inconsistent rainfall, and no real cash economy, uncertainty was the way of life for them. There was no security about tomorrow.

When I thought about my own security and reserve supplies in Nyabihanga, I painfully realized that I was *not* living like the villagers. I discovered that the difference between the poor and the not-so-poor is the opportunity to make choices. I could choose to travel by bus, truck, or private car. The poor in Nyabihanga could not. They had to travel on foot. In the morning I could leisurely delay over a second cup of coffee. The poor could not. They had to go out into the fields very early. I could order extra supplies from Rulenge. The poor could not. They had to make do with what they had. The margin of error for the poor was small. If they lost or broke an article they usually didn't have a replacement and had no money with which to buy a new one.

Yet the people in Nyabihanga seemed to manage. In rural areas of Tanzania the villagers are able to survive on very little. The deep sense of community sharing and clan loyalty direct those who are better off to help the needy.

After living in Nyabihanga for about three months, I visited Mwanza, a town of 60,000 people. The contrast between rural poverty and urban poverty was startling. The villagers were poor, but some of the city dwellers were miserable. In parts of Mwanza the congestion, open sewers, and pent-up heat created a type of oppression and inhumanity. I felt confined and weighed down by the grimness of the town. I felt stifled and bottled up. I longed for the wide open spaces of Nyabihanga. I experienced a curious, uptight feeling about the consumer society. The constant flurry of shopping, trading, and hurrying was unsettling to me. Amid all this activity and materialism I wondered what had happened to the human and personal elements. Although the residents of Mwanza had more material goods than the village people, I wondered if they had lost a deeper kind of freedom in the process. They seemed caught in the consumer system. Suddenly I wanted to be back in Nyabihanga.

These experiences challenged me to search more deeply for the real meaning of poverty and simplicity. "Poverty" is a much used and much abused word. There are many kinds of poverty: spiritual, moral, material. Certainly material poverty is not good. Lack of food, clothing, shelter, and medicine makes a person less than human, and we should try to eliminate all these kinds of material poverty so that the human family can live in dignity and freedom.

But what does poverty mean to an African? It is quite different from poverty for people of Western countries. Among many African peoples a poor man is a man who has no children, especially male heirs. A man may have a nice house, a big farm, and many material possessions, but without children to carry on his name and family line he is poor. Similarly, a poor woman is a woman who is barren. Conversely, a man may live in a wretched little hut, have a tiny farm and no animals, but if he has a houseful of children, especially boys, he is rich.

Among peoples who value cattle, such as the Wasukuma and the Wakuria, a poor man is a man without cows. Cows, more than any other material possession, are a sign of wealth. A man may have a big house, a big farm, and a great deal of money in the bank but without a herd of cows he is considered poor. Cows are especially important because they are used as the bride-wealth when the sons marry and prepare to carry on the family name.

Another African interpretation of poverty is found in one definition of *maskini*, the Swahili word for "poor." The poor person is "one who has no home or belongings." In this sense the poor person is one who has not been told the name of his or her father. This person has no claim to ancestry, no place in history, and therefore no sense of belonging to a family or a kinship group.

So just what is the Christian's call to evangelical poverty and simplicity? I searched the Scriptures for an answer. The first Beatitude says, "Blessed are the poor in spirit" (Matt. 5:3). This gospel value connotes something much deeper than material poverty. Christ calls us to be humble-minded, without a sense of self-sufficiency, aware of our ultimate need for God. Micah 6:8 describes this vocation beautifully: "This is what God asks of you: only this, to act justly, to love tenderly and to walk humbly with your God."

The stories of the Widow's Mite (Mark 12:41–44) and the Rich

Young Man (Mark 10:17–22) challenge us to examine ourselves. How far do we want to go? Part-way? Half-way? Three-quarters of the way? Christ calls us to go all the way. We should not give only from our abundance, but even from our poverty. We should not give just material goods; we should give of ourselves. Ultimately the lesson of these two gospel stories is a call to greater freedom. One of the hardest things for us to learn is that to be "beyond" money and many material needs is a freeing experience.

The prophet Isaiah gives us an insight into the gospel values of poverty and simplicity when he writes: "Share your bread with the hungry and shelter the homeless poor" (Isa. 58:7). He could have written: "Give your bread to the hungry," but he wanted to emphasize the difference between giving and sharing. It is much easier to give, especially out of one's reserve supply. To give money to a beggar on the street corner, to drop money in the Sunday collection, to support a charity appeal—these may be the easy ways out. These can be ways to salve our consciences. Giving can be an automatic gesture. As a result, we are at peace, but only for a while. There returns that nagging feeling that we have not gone far enough.

To share is much harder than to give. It demands a personal response and an involvement with the other person or persons. We have to take something of our very own, something we may need and want, and share it with our neighbor. In our contemporary world Christ is calling us to live a "parable of sharing." This is the real meaning of Christian community—to reach out to our brothers and sisters in love and service.

The description of the early Christian community in the Acts of the Apostles is a beautiful parable of sharing: "The whole group of believers was united, heart and soul; no one claimed for his own use anything that he had, as everything they owned was held in common. . . . None of their members was ever in want, as all those who owned land or houses would sell them, and bring the money from them, to present it to the apostles; it was then distributed to any members who might be in need" (Acts 4:32–35). Christ is calling our basic Christian communities of today to "go and do likewise."

When we consider our own lives, we are probably conscious of the fact that there are moments when we sympathize with the poor and the suffering, but the reality easily fades away and we find ourselves still in our own secure world. Somehow the harsh suffering of oppressed people has not burned its way into our very being, and the trials and tribulations of the little people of the world become a blurred memory. We need constant examples to remind us of this real world. Personal sickness and suffering are a help; being in touch with people on the grass-roots level is another aid in identifying with the dehumanizing poverty of so many people in the Third World. But there always seems to be an excuse for not sharing in the life of the poor and the oppressed.

The conscientization process has to begin with oneself. A simple lifestyle such as there was in Nyabihanga is one way of witnessing for liberation and justice in the world. Life in that village was basically simple. In the actual local environment I found it possible to adapt to the local food, to the lack of running water and electricity, to the lack of privacy, and to the various uncertainties of daily life. In this a supportive community was a big help.

The real test, however, is to live simply in the midst of plenty. To know that you have only beans and bananas is one thing, but to choose a simple meal from many courses in an affluent society is much harder. Evangelical poverty offers a greater challenge in highly materialistic societies and consumer-oriented cultures found in Western countries. To live a poor life in such surroundings demands spiritual motivation and discipline. This is where the support of a community is so important. The gospel value of a simple lifestyle is hard to adhere to when one struggles alone; but in a community that is living such a life there is mutual support.

My Happiest Moment
in Nyabihanga

It was late Saturday afternoon in Nyabihanga. The Little Brothers were away, but Sister Gaudiosa, from Moshi, Tanzania, was visiting us to learn about building SCCs. We walked into the garden next to the bishop's house. Christopher and John, two of the three schoolboys who lived with me, were picking gooseberries with three friends. We stood talking together. The sun was mellow in the west and cast a glow over the fields. The gooseberries were sweet. The conversation was pleasant. The sharing was deep and real. Sister Gaudiosa and the boys were enjoying the experience. So was I.

It was one of those rare moments in life that you can't plan. They just happen. There I was among a group of Tanzanians in a small, rural village—one Sister and five young boys. We experienced real Christian sharing and love. As we quietly talked and picked berries everything became clear, like a moment of revelation, like the clouds parting for the sun to burst forth. I knew why I had come to Africa, why the missionary vocation was so important to me, why friendship and sharing are at the heart of the Christian experience. It was a magical moment.

I lingered in the garden, not wanting the sun to go down, not wanting to walk back to my house, not wanting the spell to be broken. I wanted that moment to last forever.

Ever since then I have treasured that moment of love, of sharing, of Christian community. I feel that God's greatest missionary gift to me has been a deep love for the African people. They are my brothers and sisters. I feel a real part of the African family. In turn the African people have given me much love and friendship. My closest African friends have opened their hearts to me. I am deeply thankful for this precious gift and grace.

There were many other happy moments in Nyabihanga—mostly personal experiences with the African people themselves. There were times when our SCCs spontaneously reached out to help people in need—the poor, the sick, the aged. Forgetting themselves, the Christians became men and women for others. In these moments Christian love and service became real. As a community we discovered together the meaning of Christianity, and I was thrilled to be there.

Another happy moment came one day after we had been planting corn. The African Christians and I walked together back to Bukiriro to the market place. Saturday was market day and a big occasion for the villagers of Bukiriro and Nyabihanga to talk together and share the latest news. Some came to sell their bananas, sweet potatoes, or handcrafts, such as waterpots and grass mats.

Others came to buy local foods, cloth, and other goods. There was always a happy, bustling crowd. As I entered the various clusters of people I felt the joy that comes from being welcomed and accepted. Their greetings were warm and spontaneous and I felt perfectly at home.

People have asked me: What is it like to be a single white person among a crowd of Africans? After a while, differences of color, language, culture, and habits disappear into the background. One doesn't feel strange or out of place. One is simply a member of the community. A touching story is told about a missionary priest who lived for a long time in a remote part of Tanzania. He lived alone, a single white man among his African flock. One day a British government official arrived on a tour of the area. All the African children ran out to welcome the visitor. They clapped and danced. After the official left, the children excitedly told the missionary priest, "We saw a white man! We saw a white man!" A few children said that the visitor was the first foreigner they had ever seen. The priest was amazed and exclaimed, "But I'm a white man. I'm a foreigner. I've been living here with you all these years." One of the children said, "You're not a white man; you're our Father."

These happy moments in Nyabihanga reminded me of the meaning of the missionary vocation. In the seminary we learned the importance of different missionary methods: to try to get a deep understanding of the local language and culture; to proclaim the gospel in terms the local people understand; to strive for special missionary qualities such as adaptability, availability, patience, and perseverance. All these methods and qualities are important and necessary, but the basic missionary method is to love the people. Missionaries may have the finest methods and techniques, but if they do not genuinely love the people, they will fail. This love is not a paternalistic, superior type of love: "I must love those poor, backward people." It is not a general type of love: "I should love everyone." It is a self-sacrificing love and a community-centered love. In a word, it is a Christ-like love. Like Christ, we should reach out tenderly and compassionately, especially to the poor and suffering, to the forgotten people.

There is another important dimension of the missionary's love for one's people: a love for the people's culture and traditions.

Missionaries must be willing to let go of the ties to their home culture and enter wholeheartedly into their new culture. Putting up with, even adapting to, the new culture is not enough. What is required is a genuine love for the new culture, a real attempt to become one with it, not just to tolerate the newness and differences, but to appreciate and love them.

It has been said that another word for love is at-one-ness. If we truly love, we shall try to become one with that which we love. This is to imitate the love and oneness of the Trinity—Father, Son, and Holy Spirit. This idea of oneness was brought out very well on an anniversary card wishing me well in the village ministry in Tanzania: "We are like seeds and the people are like the soil. . . . Wherever we go, we should unite with them, take root and blossom among them."

A Photograph for Angelina

On returning from a trip to Nairobi I told Angelina that I had brought a present for her. Angelina, the six-year-old daughter of Angelo Bulantondera, was a frequent visitor to my house. I invited her to come with some of her friends to get the surprise. About 5 P.M. Angelina arrived with her brother, her cousin, and a few other children of the neighborhood. As they peeped in the door, I offered them a packet of colored photographs of the people in Nyabihanga village, which I had had developed in Nairobi.

The first photograph was a close-up of Angelina with her impish smile and faded red and white dress. When she saw it, she stared in amazement. When she realized it was a picture of herself, her dark brown face lit up and her big eyes danced with joy. She excitedly showed the photograph to the other children who laughed and clapped. When I pulled out other pictures of children in the neighborhood—Patricia, Mattias, Dorothea—everyone crowded around, pointing, laughing, poking each other. Soon the adults heard about the pictures and hurried over to see for themselves. When I gave Angelina's mother, Anastasia, her picture, she didn't recognize herself. She just stared at the photograph until the children pointed and shouted, "It's you! It's you!"

Many times during my two years in Nyabihanga I marveled at the excitement and joyfulness of the villagers, especially the children. When I received a packet of bubble gum I gave a piece to each of the schoolboys who lived with me and showed them how to blow bubbles. They laughed and joked and made faces as they competed with each other to see who would be the first to make a real bubble. Almost every time they made only tiny bubbles or popped holes in the gum. But they didn't care. They were having fun.

Another time I watched two girls about ten years old playing their version of jacks. Near Mulengera's hut they found a flat place in the dirt. Each girl sat on her heels, until time to kneel up for her turn. They used an old rubber ball and small stones, tossing the ball and grabbing the stones effortlessly. When I tried, I fumbled the ball on the third round. The girls smiled quietly and looked at me as if to say, "Poor Father. Don't worry, you'll get better with practice."

Angelina, the boys with their bubble gum, and the girls with their jacks have a great truth to teach. The spontaneity and happiness of young people, especially children, is a treasure the world over. The young people in Nyabihanga awakened me to the simple yet important joys of life—laughing, singing, dancing, playing games; picking tasty gooseberries in the bishop's garden on a hot afternoon; running excitedly to see the large python that was captured on the path to Bukiriro; playing soccer on a patch of dirt with a homemade cloth ball; washing school uniforms in the nearby stream on Saturday afternoon, and having more fun than work—shoving, wading, splashing.

I envied these young Africans.

Sometimes I compared these simple joys with the more "complicated" recreation or entertainment that cost a great deal of money or required expensive sports equipment, or necessitated a ride to the movie theater, or the price of a vacation many miles from home. I compared the simple delights of Nyabihanga schoolchildren with the way many children in Western society spend their free time: sitting in front of a television set for four or five hours a day or complaining that they don't have anything to do.

During my years in Africa I was constantly amazed at the Africans' happiness amid so few material goods and comforts. Now I perceive the truth of sayings such as "The best things in life are free" and "People are happy in proportion to the things they can do without." For Africans joy and happiness come from personal relationships, from sharing together. Enjoyment is in the experience, in "being" more than in "doing." It doesn't depend on material goods and things.

There is, too, a basic optimism and perseverance in the African character. Despite material poverty, little education, and frequent sickness, Africans remain hopeful and flexible. After a setback or disappointment for them, I have often heard them say, "It is nothing. We shall try again." Tested by time and outside forces, they remain confident that a new day will bring new opportunities. President Nyerere expressed this side of the Tanzanian character when he said, "We have problems, but we remain cheerful."

III
Village Life

Athanasius Misambo and I weed cabbages and tomatoes in the garden next to the bishop's house. Working together is a deep African value and essential for cooperative farming and villagization in the plan of Tanzanian socialism, or Ujamaa.

A woman fetches water from the nearby river. Villagers in Nyabihanga are typical of people in many rural, agricultural societies. The simple lifestyle fosters gospel values such as personal relationships, sharing, and serving the needs of others.

Villagers in Nyabihanga prepare the seed bed for tobacco on a day of common farming. President Julius Nyerere has said: "Most of our farming would be done by people who live as a community and work as a community. The land this community farmed would be called our land by all members."

The Many Names of Nyabihanga

Bishop Christopher Mwoleka and I had many nicknames for Nyabihanga village. Mwoleka has a great devotion to Saint Francis of Assisi. Francis is the bishop's favorite saint and special patron, whose evangelical poverty, simplicity, and humility he especially admires. Hence, when the bishop first moved to Nyabihanga in 1971 he called the village Rivototo, the name of the first friary that Saint Francis of Assisi started after he founded the Franciscan Order.

My name for Nyabihanga was "Mount Everest." Soon after I arrived in Rulenge, Brother Kees Dielemens, the treasurer general of the diocese, drove me to Nyabihanga. He told me how happy he was that the Little Brothers of Jesus and I had decided to live in Nyabihanga, but warned me that it would be a great challenge because the local people were very slow to respond to church and government initiatives. Social and economic development was still at "stage one." Kees said that our little community in Nyabihanga could be an example for the whole diocese; if we could succeed in Nyabihanga we could succeed anywhere. Nyabihanga was the supreme test. That inspired me to write the following reflection in my spiritual journal: "There are many challenges and obstacles ahead. I have nicknamed Nyabihanga 'Mount Everest.' But I am confident 'in the Lord.' The Holy Spirit is the leader of our village ministry. Under His sign we will push ahead."

We also called Nyabihanga "17 Years." To prepare for the village ministry I had lived with the Little Brothers of the Gospel in Mayo-Ouldeme in northern Cameroon. The Little Brothers arrived in Mayo-Ouldeme in 1951. There they began a life of deep spiritual presence among the Kirdi (an Arabic word referring to all the ethnic groups adhering to African traditional religions in northern Cameroon). The first Christians were not baptized until 1968—a patient waiting of seventeen years. I thought that we should be patient in Nyabihanga too. Perhaps our ministry of spiritual presence would take seventeen years to bear fruit.

After living in Nyabihanga for a short while I discovered just how inaccessible the village is. Rulenge Parish is in the far-western part of Tanzania and borders Burundi. From Rulenge town a bumpy dirt road makes a loop in the southern half of the parish. Bukiriro is nine miles along that loop, and Nyabihanga is two miles southeast of Bukiriro on a bumpier road. After a person reaches Nyabihanga there is nothing to do but turn around and go back to Rulenge town. So began Nyabihanga's other nickname: "End of the World," reminiscent of Saint Paul's words: "God has put us apostles at the end of the line" (1 Cor. 3:9). Visitors from Dar es Salaam and Mwanza often discovered the hard fact that after they made the long trip west across Tanzania to reach Nyabihanga, getting a ride back could mean a wait of several days, even a week.

But what does *Nyabihanga* itself mean? In the Shubi language *bihanga* means "skull," so Nyabihanga was the "Place of the Skull." During the two years that I lived in Nyabihanga the oldest man in the village was called Muhaya. Bent and wrinkled, he was close to eighty years old. Muhaya's parents were the first people to live in what is now the village of Nyabihanga. Muhaya himself was the first person born in Nyabihanga—around 1900. Later on Muhaya's parents were the first people to die in Nyabihanga. Following the Washubi custom they were buried near their hut. Their grave ("place of the skull") gave the village its name.

I have often thought about the meaning of Nyabihanga and what it was saying to our village ministry there. Jesus Christ was crucified on Calvary, a name that comes from the Latin word meaning the "place of the skull." Christ died on Calvary to redeem the whole human race. Perhaps our little Christian community had to go through a dying period before the village could bear fruit. Maybe the Christians in Nyabihanga were like a grain of wheat. Somehow we were all part of Christ's Paschal Mystery.

Before 1968 Nyabihanga was mainly wilderness. Only six to eight families lived in the area. The first residents, Muhaya, Nchabukoroka, and Bukobwa, told me that there were many wild animals nearby and the few families lived close together for mutual protection.

In 1968 the Tanzanian government began its vast policy of villagization in our district, which is called Bushbi. Part of the policy was to avoid overpopulation in certain areas. So from the already settled areas and existing "natural villages" every family with less than two acres under cultivation was asked to move into unsettled areas to start new villages. These new villages were called *Ujamaa* villages and followed a carefully designed government plan of development. Families from nearby villages such as Bukiriro, Rurama, Rwinyana, and Bugarama moved into Nyabihanga. Many of the people were poor and uneducated, and were looking for a fresh start. Thus Nyabihanga started officially in 1968 as a kind of "artificial village," since the original families were few. Following the influx of new people, the little community grew quickly into an *Ujamaa* village of 140 families. Nearby "natural villages" such as Bukiriro and Rurama had a Christian population of 60 percent. Since Nyabihanga began as an "artificial village" of migrant, less-educated farmers, the Christians numbered only about 30 percent of the population; the majority belonged to African traditional religions.

Nyabihanga is situated in the Ward of Bukiriro in Ngara District of the West Lake region. The population consists mostly of farmers of the Washubi people. The 1977 local census showed the following:

> 657—total population
> 137—men (also the figure for households)
> 187—women
> 162—boys
> 171—girls

The chief occupation is agriculture and the principal cash crops are beans and corn. The village is located in a series of rolling fields and scattered hills that reach a height of 5000 feet. At the foot of the hills are swamp areas used for farming during the dry season. A bumpy road runs two miles through the village until it turns into a rough, grassy track and finally into a narrow footpath. Small banana plantations and small plots of corn and beans line the road. Approximately at the center of the village is the village warehouse, a grinding machine, the political-party office, and a small shop.

When I first came to the village it looked deserted and I asked, "Where are the people?" I saw hardly any villagers except at the warehouse. In time I discovered that in the middle of each cluster of banana trees is a family house (with mud walls and a thatched roof). Each family has a small farm plot near its home together with larger plots in the common fields of the village.

Since this is a farming community, the villagers are scattered over a wide area. Narrow footpaths winding through the farmland and banana plantations bring everyone together. The village itself is divided into different sections. The Little Brothers and I lived in the northeastern section called Nyabuliga, which means "a variety of pumpkin."

Nyabihanga was by no means just a sleepy rural village. Life was never dull. Each week had its own share of surprises and dramatic happenings, of joys and sorrows: the bridge of our only road washing out during the heavy April rains; all the men and boys hunting a wild pig in a nearby field; over three hundred villagers participating in a special outdoor Eucharist to welcome four African Sisters into the village; the women's choir of Nyabihanga winning a cultural singing-and-dancing competition of all the villages in the area; the sudden and mysterious death of one of our neighbors, who was suspected of practicing witchcraft; a midnight robbery at the village store followed by an unsuccessful chase across the swamps.

Whenever I returned after a trip I would realize how much did happen in Nyabihanga. I would feel lost until I heard the latest news: births in our village; visitors from neighboring villages; decisions of the village council; an occasional death. For people living on the local level these were important and significant happenings.

The weather is generally pleasant in Nyabihanga. Lying just south of the equator, it can be fiercely hot, especially around 2 P.M., but the heat is dry and the humidity low. At our high altitude the nights are cool and ideal for sleeping, the early mornings chilly. After supper we enjoyed walking outside in the tropical evening. On clear evenings we traced the paths of the Southern

Cross, Orion, and the Big Dipper. At other times we studied the sky for the least sign of rain clouds, a ring around the pale moon usually foretelling a shower the next day.

Ujamaa Means Familyhood

One season the leaders of Nyabihanga village decided to use oxen for plowing the fields. Before getting twenty oxen from the government we had to build a cowshed. Early one morning Nchabukoroka, the leader of our ten-family cell, came to tell us that all the men in the village would work together to build the cowshed. From the bishop's community Little Brother Dominic, Joseph Mukasa, Athanasius Misambo, and I joined in. We all carried various building materials to the site—poles made from tree-trunks, grass for the roofing, nails from the workshop. In a short time we had erected the skeleton of the shed. Then we thatched the roof. Over one hundred men in the village helped in the construction. By working together we built the cowshed in a single morning.

This instance of teamwork and sharing is an example of the meaning of *Ujamaa*. The Tanzanian leaders specifically chose the Swahili word *Ujamaa* to describe and explain Tanzanian, or African, socialism, just as "humanism" was chosen to describe Zambian socialism, and other key words or "isms" were chosen to describe other philosophies and policies. According to President Julius Nyerere, *Ujamaa* "emphasizes the Africanness of the policies we intend to follow," and its literal meaning—familyhood— "brings to the mind of our people the idea of mutual involvement in the family as we know it." The foundation and objective of Tanzanian socialism is the extended family or clan. The purpose of *Ujamaa* is to spread the values of equality, solidarity, and human rights that traditionally exist in the family. *Ujamaa* is a deliberate policy of the Tanzanian government to transform the lives of the people and to bring them together into one great family.

Ujamaa socialism, or Tanzanian socialism, is a way of life, a philosophy, a statement of humanistic values, and an attitude of mind. It is opposed to capitalism and scientific or doctrinaire socialism, which have different means of production. *Ujamaa's* emphasis on human equality helps to build a classless society in Tanzania. The focus is on working and sharing together. When referring to people who do not cooperate until it is too late, Africans use a delightful proverb: "The brotherhood of coconuts is a meeting in the cooking pot."

A key to *Ujamaa* socialism in Tanzania is the policy of villagization. President Nyerere has said, "While others try to reach the moon, we are trying to reach the villages." Since 1962 the Tanzanian government has promoted village settlement programs. The Arusha Declaration in 1967 stressed the importance of people living together in villages, especially in the new settlements called *Ujamaa* villages. The purpose of villagization is to bring about a new relationship in the lives of the people, and to raise their standard of living on the basis of equality.

When people live together in villages, the government can provide them with basic community services such as running water, roads, schools, and dispensaries. There is opportunity for using modern farming methods and equipment such as grinding machines to increase production. Joint projects such as cooperative shops, brick-making, carpentry, and retail shops promote socioeconomic development. In addition, villagization stimulates political conscientization among the people so that they can understand and participate more fully in the policy of *Ujamaa*.

During the past few years the Tanzanian government has experimented with various types of villages. In theory, every village is a *Ujamaa* village "in process." In fact, very few villages have fulfilled all the government requirements and qualified as full-fledged *Ujamaa* villages. One requirement is that the villagers undertake their economic activities communally, especially farming. A second requirement is that the village must be approved by the Central Committee of CCM (Chama cha Mapinduzi, or Revolutionary party), the official party in Tanzania.

Most villages in Tanzania are "Development villages," groups that have registered and formed a village government. Many activities are done cooperatively. Each villager has his own farm and also a plot in the common field where block-farming is used. Crops are sold through cooperative stores. The major means of production are owned cooperatively. However, Development villages are only in the first stages of becoming *Ujamaa* villages.

Each Tanzanian village has its local government. The government organ in the village is the village council. If a village has a branch of the Revolutionary party, it also has five village committees, which are elected by members of the party. A diagram of the village structure (as followed by Nyabihanga and many other villages) follows:

Village Government Structure

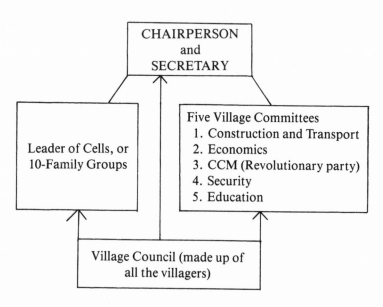

Power is vested in the people and comes from below.

In 1978 the population of Tanzania reached 16 million. Statistics on the villagization program were as follows: 13,669,162 people living in villages; 7539 villages, of which 6042 had formed local governments; 5800 village shops; 1200 cooperative shops.

During my two years in Nyabihanga I saw many changes in the evolution of *Ujamaa* and villagization. From its beginning in

1968 Nyabihanga was called a *Ujamaa* village although techni-
cally it was only in process. By 1978 the term "*Ujamaa* village"
had become less common, and we began using only "Nyabihanga
village."

One of the main reasons the Little Brothers of Jesus and I went
to Nyabihanga was to participate in the common work (*kazi ya
ushirika,* "cooperative work") and thus actually to live *Ujamaa.*
In September 1976 we joined our ten-family cell, with Nchabukoroka as our "headman." There were fifteen such cells in the
whole village, and each cell had a section in the common village
farm on which to grow beans, corn, and millet. Common work
days were Monday, Tuesday, and occasionally Thursday, with the
total work time averaging six to eight hours per week. (My blisters
made it seem like a lot more.) We cultivated shoulder to shoulder
and moved ahead in a single line—a visible sign of *Ujamaa.* Part
of the profits of the harvest went to the village, part was divided
among the members of our cell. Yet for the amount of time spent
in the common work, the profits were small, probably because the
villagers did not work as hard in the common fields as in their
individual fields. In late 1977 we shifted more and more to block-
farming, where each family had a small private plot within the
section of our cell. We continued to cultivate together, but all the
profits went to the individual families.

By 1978 the villagers preferred block-farming (more like
private enterprises) to working in the common fields. They were
given additional private plots within the overall plan of block-
farming. In addition, the government introduced the "field of the
nation" and the "field of the region." All villagers were to work
together in these fields, and all profits to go to the village store to
be used for various village needs—salaries of the village leaders,
farm equipment, tools, and various commodities. However, the
new emphasis was on volunteer work rather than requiring the
villagers to work in common. At the same time the government
started to encourage more small private businesses (mainly shops)
on the local level.

What is the church's role in *Ujamaa* and villagization? Julius
Nyerere pointed out that the Christian churches in Africa can
contribute decisively by equipping people "with sound mental attitudes and a moral outlook to participate in the task of nation-

building. . . . What we call African socialism will give the churches the opportunity to practice what they have been preaching for centuries." Bishop Mwoleka speaks in a similar vein: "I am dedicated to the ideal of *Ujamaa* because it invites all men, in a down-to-earth practical way, to imitate the life of the Trinity which is a life of sharing. . . . Only those who understand Christianity as consisting in the sharing of life in God are capable of appreciating *Ujamaa* as a God-given golden opportunity for the church to perfect its mission."

Christianity can help promote the values of *Ujamaa* at the same time that it carries out its religious mission. Sharing in the life of the people in *Ujamaa* villages is a true preaching of love for our neighbor. Mwoleka says, "The government is trying to set up social structures that are viable for this kind of life. I think it is the duty of church members to supply the interior dispositions for this kind of life."

A unique opportunity thus exists for church pastoral workers to live a ministry of presence in the villages. The new call in the church today is to work *with* the people rather than *for* them, to share the life of the people rather than merely render services to them. There is a special vocation today for priests, religious, and other pastoral workers to live in the villages and share the life of the people. A sharing and caring SCC can be a real sign of the values of familyhood.

In stressing the value of priests and religious who share the life of the people in the village, Mwoleka says:

> As we go to stay in the villages we won't have a division of two communities in one village—one community for the religious and the other for the villagers. We will be one community with them. No doubt the families [of the village] will be located here and there, but there will be a real unity among all of them. Our family [of priests and religious] will also be one among them. . . . As we have been giving ourselves to our religious community, we should now give ourselves to all members of the village and make one community together.

In the village ministry a community of pastoral workers can be the "light," "salt," and "leaven" within the wider community. I discovered a concrete example of this in the common work in Nyabihanga village. Common work is basic to the whole philosophy of *Ujamaa*—Tanzanian people working and sharing together. Yet it is a struggle for the government leaders to convince the people to work as hard (if not harder) in the common fields as in their own individual fields. Here is a great opportunity for the Christian ideals of service and unselfishness to be put into practice. Priests, Brothers, Sisters, and lay pastoral workers who live in villages can give an important witness in their dedication to the common work and other cooperative activities in the village.

As in any society, there is a certain amount of inequality, exploitation, and corruption in the implementation of *Ujamaa* socialism in Tanzania. Christians living in villages have a prophetic role and can witness to the gospel values of freedom, justice, and liberation. Jesus Christ's mission as described in Luke 4 can be applied to the village ministry. Villagers in Tanzania can (1) "Bring the good news to the poor"—the childless, the orphan, the widow, people living alone in the village; (2) "Proclaim liberty to captives"—villagers made captive by witchcraft, superstition, and traditional beliefs and taboos; (3) "Proclaim to the blind new sight"—villagers blinded by tribalism and other forms of prejudice and discrimination; (4) "Set the downtrodden free"—simple villagers oppressed by local leaders; (5) "Proclaim the Lord's year of favor"—the year of a plentiful harvest in the village.

Many people ask, "Is *Ujamaa* working in Tanzania?" to which there is a bewildering variety of answers and opinions. *Ujamaa* has its vocal supporters and critics both inside and outside Tanzania. From my experience in Nyabihanga, I would say progress in social and economic development is very slow. On a regular basis, the common fields of the village have not been successfully cultivated. The villagers work harder on their private plots than in the common fields. Modern farming methods have not succeeded yet. For example, they need more widespread use of fertilizer, more efficient planting methods (such as using rows), and ox-drawn plows. Progress is also very slow in health care (especially for children), adult education, and construction of permanent houses. It is largely a matter of the lack of motivation and felt needs, and a traditional value system that is not based on achieving a higher standard of living.

Nyabihanga has been more successful in the common-services

aspects of villagization. The villagers are conscientious in maintaining the village road. People from miles around come to use the grinding machine. The village store has increased its business. Many bags of beans and corn are sold through the cooperative store.

Concerning the overall development of the village, progress is slow. The villagers have a lot of goodwill, but find it hard to move ahead. A Tanzanian researcher who studied Nyabihanga said that our villagers suffered from four main problems: poor leadership and bad organization; lack of understanding of the responsibilities of living in a community; witchcraft, which creates fear and suspicion; and unwillingness on the part of the people to change their old ways of doing things.

When Bishop Mwoleka lived in Nyabihanga in 1972 he kept a diary of the village happenings. Subsequently, when I compared my diary of 1976–78 with the bishop's, I found that many of the same problems remained: poor planning, no cash crops on a regular basis; resistance to change and new methods; malnutrition among the children; lack of clothing; and the strong influence of witchcraft on the daily lives of the people.

In other parts of Tanzania villagization has had mixed results. On the positive side, we find that model villages have been very successful, but they have depended on expertise and resources from the outside. The policy of *Ujamaa* socialism has raised the standard of living in the poorest areas of Tanzania, such as Kigoma, by regrouping houses and providing common services. Regrouping has broken down superstition and provided geniune familyhood. Block-farming has helped the villagers to break out of the vicious circle created by having only small, individual plots. A cash economy has brought medicine, clothes, and more schools.

On the negative side, the forced movement of the Tanzanian people into villages has failed in certain areas. In the better-off areas of Tanzania, for example, in Bukoba, where cash crops such as coffee and tea already provided a stable economy, *Ujamaa* has not produced many changes. In areas where people were already living fairly close together, for example, in Moshi, villagization has not made a great impact. Many ethnic groups, for example, the Wasukuma, have opposed working together in collective farming, as this is foreign to their culture.

Tanzanian socialism is idealistic, especially as seen in the vision of Nyerere. The real test will come when these ideals are put into practice. Until now there has been a big gap between the theory and the practice. The number of people who are dedicated and committed to *Ujamaa* is relatively few. But the opportunities and possibilities for *Ujamaa* remain bright even though there are many difficulties and obstacles ahead. In stressing that Africa must travel as fast as it can in order to catch up with the modern world, President Nyerere has said, "We must run while they walk."

Slow Apprenticeship to the Real

Before washing my clothes I used to soak them overnight in soapy water. On one particular occasion as I swished the clothing, I felt something slimy on the bottom of the bucket. At first I thought it was some soap powder that had accumulated in a gooey ball, but feeling it again, I noted that the slimy thing was long and thin like a rope—and suddenly realized that it was a snake. A cold chill went up my spine as I remembered the many dangerous snakes in the area. Trembling a little, I carried the bucket outside and dumped out the water. At the bottom was a slimy black snake—dead. I breathed more easily. The snake must have fallen off the mud wall into the bucket and drowned. I was still shaking as I thought about this close call. Later Bishop Christopher told me that this particular type of snake, while not deadly, produces a festering wound that starts to heal, but then becomes inflamed again and again.

Another frightening experience occurred one day when the chairperson of the village announced that all villagers should be in their houses by six o'clock. A lion had been heard prowling around after dark in a nearby field, and they were not to take any chances. Although I never actually saw a lion during my two years in Nyabihanga, I did hear a lion roaring on a distant hill one evening. I double-checked my door and windows that night.

On another occasion I participated in a weekly Bible service in Bukiriro village. The service finished just before dusk, and as I walked back to Nyabihanga I decided that there was still enough light for me to use the shortcut through the woods and fields. But darkness closed in quickly, and when I was only halfway home, I could no longer see the path. Soon I was lost. It was too dark to retrace my steps, so I walked straight ahead hoping to meet up with the right path. Everything looked the same—the trees, the short grass, and the small footpaths that forked in all directions. The pale moon was hidden behind dark clouds. I was thoroughly lost.

Remembering what the schoolboys had told me about pythons using the footpaths at night, I imagined what would happen if I had to sleep in the bush all night. Finally I decided to strike out in the direction of the main dirt road that connected Bukiriro and Nyabihanga. After twenty minutes I reached a house in a cluster of banana trees. Joyfully I shouted a greeting, and a young boy emerged and quickly led me back to the main dirt road. The twenty-minute shortcut had turned into a two-hour adventure.

However, the physical conditions were among the easiest parts of village life. Once I visited two communities of Sisters, one African, and one missionary, who lived in other villages. When I asked them what were their major difficulties and greatest challenges, I received a variety of answers: (1) language barrier: difficulty in speaking the local languages (Kirundi, Kihangaza, and so forth), as well as the fact that very little Swahili was spoken by many of the villagers, especially the women; (2) lack of support by other priests and Sisters; (3) lack of a clear plan for the future; (4) discouragement over the slow progress experienced in helping the people to raise their standard of living and improve their farming methods; (5) the demands of living closely with only one other person; (6) sickness, especially the many infections common in the area.

My own experience was similar. My greatest disappointment in the village was in not being able to share more deeply with the people because of my limited facility in Swahili, and my lack of understanding of Shubi, the local language. Too, I felt a lack of stimulation resulting from not being able to share with the people on a deep, interpersonal level.

During my two years in Nyabihanga I often felt that God was constantly exposing me to my weaknesses, limitations, and failures: not being able to cook or fix things, getting tired quickly from the manual labor in the fields, struggling with the local language, and making so many accommodations to the ordinary village life. Yet through all this God was reminding me of a great truth that Saint Paul emphasizes in his Second Letter to the Corinthians: "We are only the earthenware jars that hold this treasure to make it clear that such an overwhelming power comes from God and not from us" (2 Cor. 4:7).

Stimulated by all this I have reflected deeply on the Parable of the (Reverse) Talent. In the traditional interpretation of this parable (Matt. 25:14-30) we are encouraged to use our talents, gifts, and special qualities and to try to multiply them. But the Parable of the (Reverse) Talent suggests something quite different. In some mysterious way God prefers to work through our weaknesses, limitations, and failures. God uses the weak to overcome that strong, the foolish to overcome the wise, the lowly to overcome the mighty (1 Cor. 1:27-28). Our weaknesses allow God to shine through us in a special way. Paradoxically, it is our unsureness (our faith), rather than our successes, that makes us strong. When we come before God humble, needy, and open, God fills us with saving power and grace.

Part of the mystery of salvation is that people reach God when God touches their sinfulness, weakness, and nothingness. God's saving power transforms our weakness. Holiness is not the opposite of sinfulness. It is through recognition of our sinfulness and limitations that we begin a pilgrimage to God, who is all-holy. Through living our humanity we experience God's life in us.

This is the way of Saint Theresa of the Child Jesus, who teaches that our weakness gives us the boldness to offer ourselves completely to God. It is only in becoming like little children that we can enter the kingdom of God (Matt. 18:3). This is also the spirituality of Charles de Foucauld, which stresses living the hidden life of Nazareth. Living and sharing with the Little Brothers of Jesus helped me to discover a new dimension of my missionary vocation, and a prayer of Carlo Carretto became very important in my life: "Teach us to be small and poor in our work and humble and hidden in life." All this is a challenge to the Western values of success, achievement, and fulfillment.

Through all these experiences I was able slowly to discover and understand the meaning of the ministry of spiritual presence. Basically it is a being rather than a doing—sharing with the people rather than a working for them and achieving. It is a seeing and a listening. The important thing is not what we do but who we are. My slow apprenticeship to the real in Nyabihanga taught me that it is one thing to live near the people, beside the people; it is a very different thing to live with the people, among the people. In a task-oriented ministry—for example, teaching school or working in an office—a person can say, "I have caught up with all my work" or "Now is the vacation period" or "Now I can get away for awhile." To a certain degree this is also true for persons working in a parish. But the ministry of presence means sharing with the people and being with the people as much as possible. There is never really a break or a holiday, because the people are always there in the village. Leaving the village for anything (even things that are good and necessary such as retreats, renewal seminars, meetings, and vacations) can only dilute the experience of completely sharing the life of the people on the local level. Thus the ministry of presence presents a challenge to one's outside commitments whether they are one's religious community, obligations to the wider church, or precautions that need to be taken to safeguard one's health, such as an annual vacation.

As new models of ministry emerge in the church today, the ministry of spiritual presence is assuming new importance. During their 1975 General Chapter the White Sisters (Missionary Sisters of Africa) expressed the meaning of their "presence" in the words "communion" and "incarnation":

> In the actual context of mission today, these are two aspects of the same reality. Presence is understood as "being with." This is a new experience of mission in which we go from the "witness of works" to the "witness of presence." No longer measured by numbers, not even by activity, it requires a quality of being that involves the whole person. Much more discreet, poor, close to the people, this form of presence calls for lighter, more mobile, less established structures and requires more creativity and discernment as well as an acculturation that should grow in depth as the Africans themselves become more aware of their own identity.

When I visited the Little Brothers of the Gospel in Cameroon, West Africa, I learned a lesson about presence. Between 1951 and 1976 only two hundred adult Christians entered the church. Yet during all those twenty-five years the Little Brothers were deeply present among the people, their people. There is a patience that says, "If I bide my time now and am patient, I will get results later on." But the Little Brothers have a deeper kind of patience, a spiritual patience. This is a total "being" with the people, a loving presence that does not look for results and achievements, a "oneness" with the people that is beyond expectations.

How can one describe this special quality of spiritual presence? Perhaps the analogy of the missionary church as fisherfolk is best. Many missionaries are involved in catching as many fish as they can. The priests, Brothers, and Sisters living in villages in Rulenge, and the Little Brothers in Cameroon, are special kinds of fisherfolk. They are more involved in the experience of fishing than in what they catch.

In the village, during common activities such as meetings, I had a concrete experience of this. Normally I find long meetings slow-moving and boring, expecially when there is a lot of discussion but little actual decision-making. In trying to "be present" in the village, however, I participated in meetings with a very different attitude and expectation. I could sit for three or four hours without getting tired. The sharing of ideas in the group was more important than the actual decisions made. Gradually I became more and more comfortable with the process of dialogue in which everyone has a chance to speak, and where the African values of personal relationships and consensus are emphasized.

The ministry of spiritual presence is an opportunity for missionaries to touch fundamental human experience in a deeper way. They live much closer to basics. They are able to experience fundamental realities through sharing with the people on the absolutely local level. Since the focus is on being rather than doing, they have more time to step back and reflect on their experiences. A heavily task-oriented life gets in the way of experiencing the more person-centered aspects of life.

At the same time, the contemplative dimension must be an important part of the ministry of spiritual presence. It is a prayer presence with prayer being a way of life rather than a series of isolated acts. It is an integration of the contemplative and the active ministries. This contemplation in action can be an experience of the Lord in a deeper way. A group of pastoral workers living in the villages expressed their vocation in these words: "Jesus Christ is the center of our lives and the center of our apostolate in the villages. Our ministry of Christian presence in the *Ujamaa* villages begins and ends with Christ."

It is good to remember that the ministry of presence can be part of a person's life wherever he or she is. It can be lived out in a city as well as in a rural area, in America as well as in Africa. It means giving priority to the personal experience more than to the task to be done. It means being available to others, on call to them.

To give a concrete example: one day I took a "presence walk" in Nairobi, Kenya. Normally I would go into Nairobi to mail a letter at the post office, buy supplies, or visit a doctor. But this particular time I decided I wouldn't try to do anything. I would just try to be—to experience the people and events of a big African city. So I merely walked around—listening to the sounds, watching the sights, and becoming involved in downtown Nairobi. I was very conscious of the activity of the city people—messengers rushing by, busy shoppers demanding immediate attention, impatient drivers honking their horns, young boys playing in the parking lots. I realized how task-oriented everyone was. As I tried to be fully present to the people and the whole city experience, I began to be more aware of the pain and suffering of people: crippled beggars holding out worn hands for a few coins, clerks and waitresses being hounded by impatient customers, lonely teenagers walking around with nothing to do. I found myself becoming more sensitive to others—a woman who dropped her package, an old man threading his way slowly through the pedestrian traffic, a blind woman crossing the street. I began to think; maybe we should occasionally step back from the hectic pace of daily life and take a "presence walk."

Within the ministry of presence are many styles of presence. The Little Brothers and Little Sisters of Jesus live a life of quiet, or hidden, presence—being present to the local people through work, prayer, and love without doing any specific apostolic activity. Other people live a prophetic presence—witnessing to the evils of injustice, poverty, and oppression. A third type is pastoral presence.

In Tanzania (and other parts of the world) I have met priests, Sisters, and other pastoral workers who are asking: How can we have a more significant pastoral presence among the people? One missionary priest in Tanzania writes:

> How is one present? By physical closeness? By service? By sharing? By leading? By walking hand-in-hand? By following? As a friend, father, or what? How does one pastor? By teaching, preaching, and celebrating the sacraments? By healing? By one's prayerfulness? By visiting? By administration? Through human development? By training local leaders?

Through villagization in Tanzania pastoral activity is shifting from the parish center to the outstations and villages. For an increasing number of pastoral workers this means living closer to the people and developing deeper relationships on the local level. Sharing with, and service to, local Christian communities is becoming more important than organizing and administrating.

Pastoral presence can throw light on the meaning of the contemporary priesthood and the whole Christian vocation. To describe priesthood in terms of function or profession (for example: to say a priest acts as a priest only while preaching, administering the sacraments, and so forth) is clearly a minimalist position. Priesthood is better described as a state of life, a total commitment of all of one's experiences. The idea of pastoral presence can help enrich the vocation of priesthood. By being present to people (available, open, listening, even vulnerable) priests are really living their ministry, even though they may not be able to measure the results in concrete achievements. The focus is on being with the people rather than doing for them.

During my two years in Nyabihanga village we often reflected on the difference between presence and service. We concluded that at certain times the ministry of presence leads to a ministry of service. (But the service must be with the people rather than just to or for them.) Many visitors challenged us for living the ordinary life of the local people without encouraging the villagers to improve their standard of living. They said we merely encouraged the status quo without promoting development goals. As a result, at one meeting of pastoral workers living in villages in Rulenge Diocese we concluded:

> We don't want always to live the exact life of the people in the villages and stop there. At times our responsibility may be to live one step ahead of our village community, to be an example in such areas as health standards, living conditions, farming methods and various innovations that will improve the "quality" of the lives of the people in our villages. So at different times we may be called to be "light," "salt," and "leaven." But we don't want to live so differently or apart from the other people in our villages that they cannot (or will not) try to follow our example. If we priests and Sisters were to take too much leadership this would harm the development of the local leadership. Decision-making for change and progress must come from the people themselves.

Many times we discovered how delicate is the balance between presence and service.

Living under the Sign of the Hoe

Every year on February 5 the villagers went to Bukiriro to celebrate the founding of the Revolutionary party (CCM), the only political party in Tanzania. Everyone gathered at the party office for speeches and the raising of the party flag. The CCM flag has a hoe and hammer in yellow against a green background. The hoe symbolizes farming and the hammer industry—signs of Tanzania's social and economic development.

In rural Tanzania we live under the sign of the hoe. As the basic implement in the fields, the hoe is the Tanzania farmer's constant companion and indispensable tool. We use the hoe to cultivate the fields, make holes to plant the seeds, weed the young plants, and harvest such crops as sweet potatoes and carrots. In addition we use hoes to scrape the road, to cut short grass, to dig pits, and even to kill snakes.

The hoe symbolizes a way of life for the Shubi farmer: the dignity of manual labor and life close to the land. Callused hands speak of honest sweat and toil under the burning tropical sun. As the village men and women cultivate in a single line they raise and lower their hoes in unison, singing as they work—a sign of *Ujamaa* and teamwork. When a man takes a second wife, he goes with her and an older female relative to his farm. The three people cultivate a small plot of land to solemnize the marriage contract. Putting aside the hoe for three days is a sign of mourning and respect for a deceased person.

In many places in Tanzania the government is introducing ox-plowing to replace the much slower method of farming by hand (using the hoe). The more modern areas use tractors. These changes are inevitable and for the social and economic good of Tanzania. Yet for the Tanzanian farmer to put aside the hoe is more than just to put aside a farm tool. It means a deep cultural and psychological change as well. For many, many years the hoe has symbolized working together and sharing together.

Again and again I discovered that one of the deepest African values is doing things together. Africans often prefer achieving a little together to achieving a lot individually. Emphasis is on the group and the community experience. To break ground in a new section of the village fields, the men work together, not separately. For volunteer work in the village, such as scraping the road or digging up rocks for the foundation of the enlarged church, it is easier to get fifty people to participate than only five. Everyone wants to feel part of the common activities.

One day one of our Christian leaders, Petro Bujali, walked for forty-five minutes from his home on the outskirts of Nyabihanga to the church in Bukiriro. He had volunteered to help dig the foundations of a badly needed latrine near the church. When his partner failed to show up Petro refused to dig, saying that he would work in a team or not at all. So he returned home. A Westerner would say that the day had been wasted, since nothing had been accomplished. But Petro was witnessing to a basic human value in African culture.

This incident prompted me to reflect on sharing as the Christian way of life too. One Maryknoll Sister who lived in a village in Rulenge Diocese explained her spiritual motivation in these words:

> We, as religious, are not called to live apart from other people, to live a life that separates us from them. Christ never gave us that example. Rather, we live in the midst of people, sharing sufferings, longings, and joys, conscious of the great mystery of sharing God's life and love. . . . Our response to this call leads us to enter fully into the village community, to struggle through the daily hard work of farming people, to experience insecurities together, to strive to improve the living conditions of all—not to live as a privileged class—but to cast our lot with the poor.

Another Maryknoll Sister described her village experience this way: "This is the most exciting part of living in the village: having the perspective of the villagers become to some degree your own, and sharing life then in a whole new way, with a whole new appreciation of gospel values."

The Little Sisters of Charles de Foucauld lived in Ruganzu village in the eastern part of Rulenge Diocese. Throughout the world their basic vocation is to share the ordinary life of the people, the working-class people. One Little Sister told me that they do not try to live a life of poverty as such, but they live in whatever circumstances the people live—be it Ruganzu, Nyabihanga, or New York. Their "contemplative-in-the-world" vocation is to identify with people on the local level, imitating the hidden life of Jesus at Nazareth.

Jesus Christ brought about our redemption through an incarnation. He did not stand aside from us but entered into his creation. In assuming our nature Jesus took on our human condition including all the hazards of life and even the guilt for our sins. The Son of God truly became the Son of man. He shared our life. We translate a passage in the prologue of Saint John's Gospel as "And the Word became flesh and dwelt among us" (John 1:14), but this passage is more accurately translated as "And the Word became flesh and pitched his tent among us." Today a man or woman may dwell among us without sharing the hazards of life that beset the ordinary person. He or she may live in a penthouse in a restricted neighborhood, eat in exclusive restaurants, play at select country clubs, and travel in staterooms. Such persons may never enter a ghetto or a slum, never stand in line at a cafeteria, never ride a bus. We can say that, after a fashion, they dwelt among us. But they did not pitch their tent among us.

Jesus truly pitched his tent among us. He set the norm for all ministries, for all redemptions. In Tanzania the *"Ujamaa* Jesus" called us to share the life of the village people. He challenged us to incarnate ourselves fully in the everyday life and culture of the people on the local level.

Bishop Mwoleka stressed again and again that the heart of the gospel is sharing life in all its aspects. He says: "The essence of Christianity is SHARING OF LIFE. . . . In our *Ujamaa* country, therefore, Christians should distinguish themselves by being exemplary in the life of sharing with others and overcoming selfishness."

By living full time in Nyabihanga village our little community of pastoral workers was able to share the everyday life of the people from the inside—to share their joys and sorrows, their problems and uncertainties, their hopes and dreams. We were able to touch the lives of the villagers more deeply and be touched by them. We were fully accepted as members of the village community. This had enormous implications for our ministry. One Sister said, "One must be seen as brother or sister in order to evangelize in depth." Not only did we evangelize as "insiders," but we ourselves were evangelized by the local people.

Though we priests, Brothers, and Sisters made great efforts to share with the local people, the Christian example of Athanasius Misambo, a Sukuma layman, seemed to outshine our efforts. One day when Bishop Christopher came to Nyabihanga on an unexpected visit, we hurriedly tried to prepare tea for the villagers who came to greet the bishop. Soon we had finished our two thermoses of tea. Finally the bishop, Athanasius, and I were left sitting together. I wondered what I would do if another visitor came. Just then one of our neighbors did arrive to say hello to the bishop. As I started to apologize for not having any tea, Athanasius spontaneously picked up his own cup of tea and politely handed it to the visitor. It was a simple gesture of sharing, but for me a profound act of love and beauty. By his example Athanasius had evangelized me.

Following the Bean Cycle

One autumn, the lay leaders of Bukiriro outstation decided to expand the church farm. The government gave us a one-acre plot in an uncultivated area of the village. We planned to raise beans and corn, and asked each SCC to volunteer workers for one Saturday morning every month. (The profits would go into the church treasury and be used to help the poor and needy.)

The actual schedule went like this:

November: Dig up the tree stumps and cut the grass and weeds. With an ox-drawn plow, do the initial cultivation.
December: Cultivate by hand.
January: Plant corn.
February: Weed the corn.
March: Plant beans.
April: Weed the beans.
May: Sleep in the field at night to guard against wild pigs.
June: Harvest the beans.
July: Shell the beans. Harvest the corn.
August: Shuck the corn. Sell the beans and corn.

I shall always remember the ten long months of patient work; the many days of getting up in the cold wetness of a dark Saturday morning; the half-hour walk to Bukiriro, and a further forty-five minutes to the church farm on the outskirts of the village; the villagers suddenly appearing ghostlike out of the morning mist, a single file of shadows carrying hoes; the joyous greetings as we met at the main path, a chorus of happy voices echoing across the still valley. Each SCC had a small section of the church plot, but we worked together and pooled all the beans and corn during the harvest season. When the Christians decided to use part of the money from the sale of the beans and corn to help needy people, my joy was full.

Following the bean-and-corn cycle helped me to get into the rhythm of the farming life of the villagers, who are truly people of the land. Agriculture is the center of their life. As President Nyerere said, Tanzania's greatest resources are its people and its land.

The Little Brothers and I participated in the common work of our ten-family cell on Mondays and Tuesdays. It was easy to be deceived about the actual amount of work done. We used twenty to thirty minutes just walking to the fields, and during the rainy season we had to run for cover often. I calculated that in my first six months in Nyabihanga I did common work on the village farm on twenty-three different days. Yet the actual working time was only fifty-six hours, or nineteen minutes per day during the six-month period. My sore back made it seem like a lot more time.

In addition to the common work we had our own small fields and gardens as part of the bishop's farm. Little Brothers Marcel and Dominique were experienced farmers and spent hours on our farm every day. As a novice, I just managed to keep up with a small garden in which we planted lettuce, tomatoes, carrots, cabbages, onions, and gooseberries. I had mixed success. I failed when the sun was too hot and the vegetables dried up, or when the rain was too heavy and the plants spoiled, or when caterpillars ate the gooseberries, or when goats and rabbits got in.

I shall always remember Friday, December 31, 1976, as "The Day I Ate My First Carrot from Our Garden." The small (and I emphasize *small*) carrots we harvested from our garden were the first food that I had personally planted and taken care of. It was a milestone in my life at Nyabihanga. I had finally made it on my own.

My favorite crop was pumpkins. We could plant the seeds at random, and the green leaves would grow quickly without any weeding or extra work. Around my house in the month of January the ground was like a lush green carpet with all the holes and ugly patches covered; and the pumpkins tasted so good, especially when cooked with beans.

Working with Tanzanian farmers was a genuine learning experience for me, learning about them, or, what was more important, learning from them. Besides farming skills, I learned much from the personal qualities of the villagers themselves. The African value of sharing and togetherness was manifested many times in their farming customs. If a neighbor or visitor came by when we were planting beans or corn, the person would join us for a few minutes to help plant the seeds.

An underlying quality of the villagers was patient endurance. Rain or shine they would go to the fields. Without a complaint they would suffer through all the troubles of a farmer—burning sun, pouring rain, unexpected changes in the weather, insects, bad soil. They possessed that underlying strength of the farmer who has experienced all kinds of conditions. They had a staying power that helped them endure all the good and bad things that happened.

A sense of joy often accompanied this characteristic of patient endurance. Many times I marveled at the cheerfulness of the villagers when they were in pain. Pregnant women smiled graciously. Old men hobbling around on sore legs always had a pleasant greeting. Salvatori always seemed sick—malaria, stomach trouble, infections—yet he remained calm and cheerful even in the most trying circumstances.

I discovered among the farmers an interesting combination of optimism and pessimism. Basically they were a hopeful people with a "tomorrow is another day" attitude; but they revealed, too, a kind of resignation and fatalism regarding the weather, their crops, and sickness in the area. They would always remind me that too little rain and too much rain could spoil our crops. I had the feeling that by lowering their expectations for a good harvest the villagers were protecting themselves from disappointments. They didn't like to anticipate success—as though it might bring bad luck.

The soil of our church farm was rich, and the young beans and corn grew quickly. After weeding the beans and corn for the last time, I asked our outstation chairperson, Petro Gwanka, what kind of harvest we could expect. He refused to answer, saying that it was dangerous to make predictions. He would only mention possible problems such as wild pigs eating the fresh corn. The villagers were almost superstitious in not wanting to talk about the harvest until all the work was finished.

As I tried to enter more fully into the lives and values of the people, I listened to the proverbs the people used most frequently in my effort to discover which proverbs were most deeply embedded in the life and culture of the local people. Many proverbs related to the "slow but sure" theme necessary for a farmer:

A slow rain bears the most fruit.

Hurry, hurry, has no blessing.

Little by little fills up the measure.

Better delay and get there.

Chip! chip! finishes the log.

A person who is too much in a hurry stubs a toe.

A slow, steady walk carries one far.

These proverbs describe very well a basic attitude in the local people. They were never in a hurry. Salvatori often told me, "What we don't do today we will do tomorrow." Of course this philosophy had its negative side. To delay planting after the first heavy rain or to be too slow to take a sick child to the dispensary often produced additional problems and uncertainties.

Eating Lunch at 8 P.M.

Before living in Nyabihanga I had never done any cooking beyond boiling water and making popcorn. In the village I volunteered to share the cooking with the two Little Brothers, Marcel and Fabian. I didn't realize what I was in for! Neither did the Little Brothers! The whole day was a comedy of errors. As I look back now, I think I should have made it a fast day.

I started at 10:30 A.M., planning to serve lunch at 1 P.M. The menu was rice with a meat-stock sauce and a salad from our own garden. Not having had much experience with a wood fire, I decided to cook with a charcoal stove. Unwisely I used our pressure cooker. I spent the first hour reading the directions so the lid wouldn't blow off on my first attempt. I lit the charcoal fire, using more kerosene than I should have. I washed the rice. Then I was ready to cook. The directions said that boiling the water and cooking the rice would take about fifteen minutes, so I confidently expected to reach my 1 P.M. target.

I set the sauce aside and put the pressure cooker on the charcoal fire. I waited for the steam to come up before starting to time the rice. Fifteen minutes passed and nothing happened. I discovered that the fire wasn't hot enough, so I added more charcoal and doused it with kerosene. During the next half hour I kept fiddling with the fire, but it still wasn't hot enough for the pressure cooker to work properly. At 1:30 P.M. I warned the Little Brothers that lunch would be late.

For the next hour I continued to work with the fire. When it finally got hot, the pressure cooker was still not producing the necessary steam. Several times I had to put the sauce back on the charcoal fire to keep it hot.

Around 2:30 P.M. the elderly catechist Salvatori arrived to discuss plans for our outstation, so I dropped everything to talk with him. When I returned to the kitchen an hour later, the sauce was lukewarm and the fire barely smoldering. I hadn't stirred the coals properly so the heat didn't spread evenly in the charcoal burner. When I told the Little Brothers that there would be another delay, they told me not to worry. They knew that it was important for me to succeed on my own so they decided not to help.

For the first time I admitted to myself that there wouldn't be any lunch. I tried again to make the charcoal fire hotter. Another hour passed. The coals were burning well, but the fire still wasn't hot enough to get the steam up. My small (very small!) consolation was that I had reheated the sauce.

By 5 P.M. I was close to despair. I knew that I would have to stop everything and prepare the 5:30 P.M. Eucharist for the Christians in Nyabihanga. I told the Little Brothers that we would skip our afternoon meal and have a big supper after the Eucharist.

Then things went from bad to worse. Since the Eucharist was in another house about two hundred yards away, I suddenly had a vision of the charcoal fire getting out of control and burning down the kitchen. So I threw water on the coals. This solved the fire problem but also meant that when I returned at 6:30 P.M. I had to start the charcoal fire again.

By 7:15 P.M. the charcoal fire was hot, and so were the Brothers. Naturally they were hungry and a bit impatient. I didn't have time to think about my empty stomach. Fabian came to my rescue. He quickly started a wood fire and cooked the rice while the sauce remained hot on the charcoal fire. That night we ate lunch at 8 P.M. I was immediately removed from the cooking rotation.

There and then I decided to go to Rulenge Parish and to the Maryknoll Sisters in Katerere village for cooking lessons as well as lessons in starting different kinds of fires. After twelve days I got my beginner's license. I still had trouble starting a wood fire quickly, but most of the time I managed to muddle through. I was again ready to enter the cooking rotation with the Little Brothers.

Cooking every third week was a good experience for me and gave me many insights into village life. It was another way of participating in the everyday life of the people. As I had already discovered, cooking can take up a lot of time. Cooking beans on a wood fire takes two to three hours. Collecting firewood and peeling bananas is time-consuming. I had a new respect for the Washubi women who do all the cooking besides taking care of their children and working in the fields. In fact much of an average day was taken up with ordinary tasks—cooking, cleaning, and washing.

In the village, cooking and farming were closely linked. Before cooking we would have to go to our garden to pick lettuce, carrots, tomatoes, onions, and different kinds of fruits, or into our nearby field to dig up potatoes. The green cooking-bananas came from the small plantation that was located just outside our kitchen door. A great deal of time was spent preparing the different types of food before the actual cooking of them. In learning how to cook I learned a lot about farming too. In the course of farmwork I became more familiar with the way the various crops would later be used in cooking. I learned the difference between planting string beans, which we ate fresh, and small beans that we could dry and store for several months. All this helped me to get into the rhythm of a rural farming community.

Even though the diet in Nyabihanga was simple, there was an opportunity to prepare the food creatively and maintain a balanced diet. The staple food was bananas. Besides the three main kinds—the green cooking-banana, the yellow sweet-banana, and the green beer-banana—there were many other varieties. An African bishop from Bukoba told me that the Haya people have eighteen ways of preparing bananas. He asked me how Americans eat bananas. I explained how we slice bananas over cold cereal, and how we make a banana split using bananas, ice cream, and topping. The bishop's eyes lit up as he exclaimed, "Ah, now we have twenty ways!"

My cooking experience helped me to understand self-reliance, a quality that the Tanzanian government policy stresses. The lifestyle of the Tanzanian farmer is geared toward self-reliance: cooking, farming, building, and repairing. The people are thrown back on their own resources. As a nation of farmers Tanzania is trying to increase its agricultural production and grow more and more of its own goods. President Nyerere has written:

> Self-reliance is not some vague political slogan. It has meaning for every citizen, for every group, and for the nation as a whole. A self-reliant individual is one who cooperates with others, who is willing to help others and be helped by them, but who does not depend on anyone else for his food, clothing or shelter. He lives on what he earns, whether this be large or small, so that he is truly a free person beholden to no one.

Ujamaa socialism aims for self-sufficiency in the production of proper food, suitable clothing, good housing, basic education, and adequate health facilities. The basic thrust is from the bottom up. If each person is self-reliant, then each village will be self-reliant. Only then will each district and each region be self-reliant. Finally the whole nation will be self-reliant.

The economic goal of Tanzania's program of self-reliance is increased production. Nyerere, who is called "teacher" by the people, explains this process through an ancient proverb: "Give a man a fish and he has food for one day. Teach him how to fish and he has food for every day." This self-reliance gives a person dignity and a sense of personal worth.

However, self-reliance does not mean individualism. A story is told about a man who was driving along a dirt road in Tanzania. He came upon another man whose car had broken down. The stranded man asked for help, but the passerby said, "Fix the car yourself. You should learn to be more self-reliant." But, as Nyerere has said, real self-reliance is closely linked to cooperation and sharing. The policy of villagization encourages the Tanzanian people to be self-reliant as a community. It is hoped that living in *Ujamaa* and Development villages the people will increase production and thereby raise their standard of living.

In a corresponding way the church in Tanzania and in other parts of Africa is striving to become a self-reliant church where all the basic structures and resources are found within itself. Just as in the government plan, the church's plan of self-reliance is based on the principle of subsidiarity. If the lower levels (the SCCs and outstations) are self-reliant, then the higher levels (parish, diocese, and country) will be self-reliant. Christians through their own resources must take the responsibility for the basic and ordinary service of each local community.

As I lived these experiences with cooking and other aspects of self-reliance I reflected on certain basic Christian values. The Christian vocation is to imitate Christ. In the Gospels Christ is described as a carpenter and as a cook. He was truly a man of the people. He lived in solidarity with working-class people. He did menial jobs. He wasn't afraid to dirty his hands. He served others.

The Gospel of Saint John tells a touching story about Jesus appearing to his disciples on the shore of the Sea of Galilee. After a long night of fishing, Peter and six of the disciples came ashore with their nets bulging with fish. Jesus had prepared a charcoal fire and was cooking fish. He asked for more fish. Then he said to his disciples, "Come and have breakfast" (John 21:12). The humanness of Christ shines through. He is ready to serve others. His example is a challenge to Christians everywhere.

Rainstorm at Midnight

One year the rains stopped in early May. This was a catas-
trophe. The late April rains had fallen as usual and the beans had
sprouted. During the first week of May there were two light rains,
then nothing. It was an abrupt change, like rolling a ball on a
table, then seeing it disappear off the far end. Each morning and
evening we searched the sky for rain clouds. The few dark clouds
circled our valley like cautious visitors reluctant to enter.

The men in Nyabihanga grew worried. Had the long rains
stopped early? Would this be an unusually dry May? Everyone
knew that if we reached June without rain the dry season would
continue until August. On May 24 Angelo told me that the beans
of our SCC field were beginning to dry up. The once green leaves
had started to shrivel up in the blazing tropical sun. Without rain
our harvest would be cut in half.

That night I searched the eastern horizon and saw a few dark
clouds, but no real movement in the sky. I went to bed resigned to
another day without rain. But in the middle of the night I heard
the patter of rain on our tin roof. I jumped out of bed excitedly
and flicked on my flashlight. It was 11:58 P.M. God has heard our
prayers, I thought—rain at midnight. I threw open the wooden
frame window and peered out. The gentle patter gradually turned
to a steady rain. The beans, I thought, the beans! The beans
would be saved. Thomas and John woke up too. We walked outside relishing the life-giving rain as it streamed down our faces.
We filled several tin buckets with rainwater from the gutters attached to our tin roof. Then we contentedly watched the large
metal drum (which held about sixteen buckets) start to fill up
from the glorious water pouring off the roof.

That day it really rained! During the nineteen hours from midnight to 7 P.M. there were at least ten periods of rain of varying
length. We filled over three large drums. Little Brother Marcel
remarked that one day we were conserving each precious cup of
dirty river water, and then the next day we had buckets and buckets of clean rainwater.

The midnight rain lifted the spirits of everyone in Nyabihanga.
We all knew that this good, soaking rain would produce a fine

bean harvest. There would be enough food for the long dry season. "God has blessed us," one villager said.

I never tired of watching the rain approach. I would face east as scattered gray clouds formed on the horizon. The wind would pick up as the clouds moved closer. A sudden chill would penetrate the air and my nostrils would quiver. In the next valley the rain would begin and advance toward us like a battalion of victorious soldiers marching across the battlefield. In less than five minutes bright sunshine would turn into cold, biting rain, sounding like a waterfall, growing in force as sheets of rain poured into our valley. The rain gave a whole new life and energy to the people and the land. For the villagers rain was life and the key to survival.

Psychologically, the dry season had the opposite effect. You could "feel" the dry season coming on, and this affected your attitude and spirits. You longed for rain and watched intensely for every cloud and sign of wind. You cut down on washing and cleaning; everything requiring water was reduced to the basic essentials.

During the dry season the Little Brothers and I had a lot of extra work. We walked one quarter of a mile to a small river to haul its dirty water in buckets. The thirsty vegetables cried out for a drink, but we could water the garden only sparingly. We boiled and filtered all the water used for drinking and cooking. A whole new dynamic operated. Every action was based upon the amount of water it would take, or on how much time we could spare to haul water.

For the Tanzanian farmer rain is life. It is a blessing from God, God's gift to his people. While rain is necessary for life everywhere in the world, I found that an agricultural society depends absolutely upon rain. It is the farmer who suffers most from the unpredictableness of the weather. When a person is not directly dependent on the land, rain can be a nuisance or an inconvenience. It makes driving miserable, spoils the Sunday picnic, cancels the ballgame. But to the people who are farmers rain is a gift of life.

During the rainy season in Tanzania the brown earth comes to life. In April and May the green fields of beans, corn, and millet seemed to engulf our houses and paths. As the young vines and plants shot up, we swam in a green sea of bean shoots, fresh-smelling grass, and a variety of shrubs. Rich purples, dark greens, whites, and yellows painted the tropical African landscape.

More than anything else rain gave me an insight into the meaning of uncertainty. In Nyabihanga the rain pattern was unpredictable and varied from year to year. The fall planting season always started after the first heavy rain. In my first year in the village we began planting on September 25, while in the second year we started on November 2. At a certain time in the farming cycle we would feel a great longing and need for moisture. The crops would be burning up in the torrid sun and the whole harvest would be in danger. If heavy torrents fell steadily for two weeks the farmers would say, "Now we are getting too much rain. If these hard rains continue, our crops will be spoiled." Thus the possibility of too little rain or too much rain made everything uncertain.

So I shared the uncertainty of the Tanzanian farmer and farmers everywhere. Uncertainty is the condition of men, women, and children throughout the world, but the poor and oppressed suffer the most.

I came to realize that there are at least two ways of dealing with uncertainty. One way is to fight uncertainty and try to overcome it. This means trying to answer all the questions, solve all the problems, clear up all the doubts, close off all the loopholes. Often we do this by methodical planning and organization: confirming air tickets, investing in health insurance, laying in a reserve supply of food and drink. A second way is to live with the uncertainties—to grow within them and become in harmony with them; to make them an opportunity rather than an obstacle.

This second way is to live the ministry of uncertainty, the ministry of insecurity. Most men, women, and children live lives of endless uncertainty and insecurity—"lives of quiet desperation," in the words of Thoreau. We too can enter into this deep human experience and share this hard condition of humankind, as Jesus and his disciples identified with ordinary working-class people in the uncertainty of daily living. Jesus said, "The Son of Man has nowhere to lay his head" (Luke 9:58). He challenged his disciples to give up everything to follow him. As he sent out the twelve apostles to proclaim the kingdom of God, he said to them: "Take nothing for the journey: neither staff nor haversack, nor bread, nor money, and let none of you take a spare tunic" (Luke 9:3). Finally in the agony in the garden Jesus committed himself to the uncertainty of the future as he gave himself into the hands of his Father. These gospel values of uncertainty and insecurity challenge us today.

Life in Nyabihanga taught me something else, too: not to take life too seriously. I found it helpful to accept uncertainty with a sense of humor. The communications system of Nyabihanga remained a great mystery to me. Getting the exact news of the plan for the common work or a village meeting was nothing less than a great adventure. Even Bishop Mwoleka was baffled by the "osmosis process" of communicating news in the village. One weekend we received successive news that on Monday morning we should (1) attend a meeting at 9:30 A.M.; (2) work in the southern cornfield; (3) work in the northern cornfield; (4) do nothing. We finally ended up walking for fifteen minutes to the bean field. After two minutes of digging I was called to a meeting at the other end of the village. We waited two and a half hours for the meeting to start.

This uncertainty about activities in the village was clearly my problem. My neighbors always seemed to know what was going to happen. When I explained my predicament they would shrug their shoulders and apologize—not really understanding why I was confused. Then we would laugh together.

So I tried to live with a sense of humor and sense of wonder. And life in the village went on gloriously.

A Christmas Beer Party

One Christmas afternoon Bishop Mwoleka and the Little Brothers drove to Rulenge to attend a party for the priests, religious, and lay volunteers. I decided to stay in Nyabihanga to celebrate Christmas with the villagers. Together with the three schoolboys I visited some of our neighbors, and around 6 P.M. I walked toward Merita's house. Merita was one of the staunchest Christians in Nyabihanga and loyal to Nyabuliga SCC. As I walked along I could hear singing, laughing, and shouting. It was a Christmas beer party.

After welcoming me on my arrival, the men led me to the circle of elders. They handed me a long reed and invited me to drink from a large pot of banana beer. I was to take a sip, then pass the reed to the man on my right. The reed passed around the circle and soon it was my turn again. The men clapped as I drank and said, "We are happy you have joined us. Thank you for coming."

While the drinking continued, a large circle was formed to watch the women dance. The villagers were lighthearted and talkative, for Christmas was one of the biggest celebrations in the village. Only a small group had attended the morning Eucharist, but everyone attended the beer party.

A beer party is the Washubi's main entertainment and celebration. It combines drinking, conversation, storytelling, singing, and dancing. The Shubi farmers have few diversions. Many would describe their lives as routine, even dull. The beer party is the chief social event. It is an occasion to exchange news and discuss the village happenings. The men will sit for hours around a large pot of beer—puffing on their pipes, sipping the beer, and talking.

One villager told me that the Washubi are very poor and have little to offer a visitor. Food is scarce. Without sugar the villagers feel embarrassed to offer the local tea (usually made by boiling tea leaves, milk, and sugar together). So the Washubi offer visitors beer. The most common kind is banana beer made from bitter green bananas, which have to ripen first. It is very strong and can leave quite a hangover. Second to banana beer is millet beer. When I asked my next-door neighbor, Richard, what kind of beer he liked best, his eyes lit up, he smiled broadly, and answered, "I like all kinds."

Saturdays, Sundays, and holidays are the main days for drinking beer. In the afternoons of these days men and women walk around the village to visit their friends and neighbors and search for beer. While the dried millet can be stored for months, beer bananas ripen at specific times. They have to be picked, mashed, mixed with water and left to ferment for several days. Preparing these beer bananas on Thursday means a happy weekend of drinking.

For the men in Nyabihanga drinking is part of life. One morning at 7:30 I arrived at Nchabukoroka's house to go to the common field of our ten-family cell. First he invited me into his house to drink millet beer, which has plenty of nutrition. Nchabukoroka said to me, "We need to get extra energy for our farmwork." Another day I joined the neighbors to plant beans in our section of the village farm. After the work Richard invited me for a "tea break" at a neighbor's home. Our tea was millet beer.

However, even if there is no beer to drink, the local people like to visit friends and neighbors; they enjoy receiving visitors too. Visiting is part of the African's person-centered way of life. When I traveled to other parts of East Africa I often experienced the importance of visiting. During a trip to Nairobi I called on a close friend, Mrs. Jael Mbogo. She was not in her office, so I left a note asking her to call me around 7 P.M. That same evening she arrived at the priests' residence where I was staying. She said, "After such a long time I couldn't just telephone you. I wanted to greet you in person."

Jael believes in personal contact. Busy as she is, she always has time to talk for ten minutes with any friends she meets on the street. When she arrives thirty minutes late at an important meeting, the chairperson explains, "Jael must have met three people along the way."

During a trip to Kampala, Uganda, I received a message that the mother of Joseph Mukasa Balikuddembe wanted to meet me. Joseph, a layman working in the communications media, and I had been friends for many years. When he went to the United States for advanced studies, I visited him during my long vacation. When I saw Joseph's mother, she said to me, "I'm so excited to see you because you have seen my son with your own eyes."

These African values of visiting and personal contact have important implications for our missionary and pastoral work. They give the missionary the opportunity to discuss the personal lives of the Christians, their family situations, and their various concerns. During this informal contact I discovered a great deal about the Christian life in our outstations, about certain problems in the village that formal contact at the church or in meetings would never have revealed—sensitive areas such as the unhappiness of a devout Christian woman when her husband takes a second wife and the great influence of witchcraft on the local Christian community.

Personal contact is an important part of ministry anywhere. A survey was taken among Catholics in a large Nairobi parish. One question was: "What should the priests emphasize more in the parish?" The most frequent answer was: "More home visits."

IV
Small Christian Communities

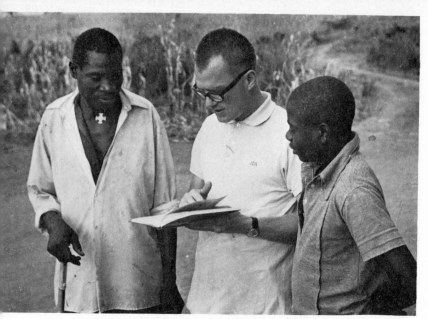

Angelo Bulantondera, the prayer leader of our small Christian community, Thomas Kidende, the treasurer, and I prepare the gospel reading for our weekly Bible service. The SCCs foster the rapid development of lay leaders and a deeper sense of the local church.

Each week the Bible service is conducted at a different home. Members of the SCC prepare a suitable place. The Christians enjoy the informality of praying at their homes. It is also a social occasion that shows African values of hospitality, fraternity, and community. Everyone is welcome including those who belong to African traditional religions.

One of the leaders reads the gospel twice, once in Swahili and once in Shubi, the local language. The SCCs promote a variety of lay leaders including song leaders, religious formation leaders, marriage counselors, promoters of self-reliance, promoters of community spirit, and animators of sacraments and spirituality.

Members of two SCCs in Bukiriro build a new home for a poor widow as part of the weekly practical action. At the heart of the meaning and purpose of SCCs is the praying community that reaches out in loving service. As Bishop Mwoleka says: "Christianity is living for others."

The Bishop's Community

Every Tuesday afternoon we attended Bible services in the SCCs in Bukiriro village. I might go to Katelama prayer group, Athanasius to Bukiriro B prayer group, Sister Veronica to Rubanga prayer group, and so on. We arrived back in Nyabihanga at different times—7:30, 8, 8:30 P.M.—and would not being supper until the last person had returned. Athanasius said, "It's good for us to eat together." Sometimes I would get impatient waiting for the others, especially when I was the cook and had to keep checking on the food, but the Sisters and laymen said that the sharing together was the important thing, and they were right!

During my two years in Nyabihanga, outsiders often wanted to know what kind of community I lived in. I found it impossible to describe our living situation—to explain the various communities of religious and lay people and the arrangement of our two houses; so I suggested that people come and see for themselves. Yet I realized it was not just a matter of "come and see" but of "come and share." Other people could best understand our community by actually sharing the experience.

What we called the bishop's farm covered some four or five acres and included two houses about two hundred yards apart. For the first year and a half the Little Brothers—Marcel, Fabian, Dominique, and Emanuel—used one house. I lived in the other house with the three schoolboys and various laymen who joined the bishop's community from time to time—Joseph Mukasa, Athanasius, Mzee Patrice. When the Little Brothers moved to another village in Rulenge Parish, four Bernadette Sisters came to live in Nyabihanga. There was a great mixture of people and backgrounds, yet whatever the groupings, the focus was always the same—to live and share together. We genuinely tried to be a complete, integrated, Christian community: priests, Brothers, Sisters, lay people; married (although the two married men came only for short periods of time while their wives and children stayed in their home villages) and single; old and young.

We tried to be a horizontal rather than a vertical comunity with shared responsibilities and ministries. We took turns cooking, cleaning, and washing as well as leading our daily Bible service, singing, and other prayers. Everyone helped in the farm work and community needs, such as fetching water and firewood.

Living in such a community was a new experience for me. Most of my life I had been used to a vertical system of living, based on authority (a hierarchy of ranks) and money (salaried workers providing services). In fact, most people live in this system. We are constantly served by a system of cooks, waiters, laundry workers, secretaries, telephone operators, drivers.

A horizontal lifestyle of sharing in common creates a very different dynamic. What made the bishop's community in Nyabihanga especially meaningful to me was the sharing with lay people. In our little community there were no clearly defined distinctions between religious and laity. We were all Christians living and sharing together. I felt a deep bond with Athanasius, Joseph Mukasa, Patrice, and the others who joined us from time to time. We were like brothers. They taught me by their example and dedication much more than I taught them.

Our community in Nyabihanga (and similar communities in other villages in Rulenge Diocese) was part of a great dream of Bishop Mwoleka's: his hopes that the small integrated community can be the basis for all Christian life and work. During our retreats, seminars, and leadership-training programs he often cited as a model the first Christian communities in the Acts of the Apostles:

These remained faithful to the teaching of the apostles, to the brotherhood, to the breaking of bread and to the prayers. The faithful all lived together and owned everything in common; they sold their goods and possessions and shared out the proceeds among themselves according to what each one needed (Acts 2:42–46).

The whole group of believers was united, heart and soul; no one claimed for his own use anything that he had, as everything they owned was held in common. . . .None of their members was ever in want, as all those who owned land or houses would sell them, and bring the money from them, to present it to the apostles; it was then distributed to any members who might be in need (Acts 4:32–35).

Bishop Mwoleka hopes that priests, Brothers, Sisters, laymen, and laywomen can live, work, and pray together in a horizontal community of shared tasks and ministries. Pastoral workers would live gospel values and share life in a mixed or integrated community (covenant communities including married households). Mwoleka says:

> If there is a healthy attitude that is all-pervasive in the church today, it is the conviction that the Christian life must be lived in community. Many stress more life in small Christian communities—where each one must be involved in the lives of every other. It is not one of many ways—it is *the* way. In the genuine Christian community we must find men and women, old and young, married and single, learned and simple, healthy and sick, professional and the common, ordained and lay. These should live not adjacently or in juxtaposition, but their lives, charisms, talents, and shortcomings must be integrated to form a single whole and function like an organism.

Part of Mwoleka's dream is that the integrated community model be extended to all parts of Rulenge Diocese—villages, parishes, training centers, and diocesan centers. He hopes that all parishes can be based on the Acts of the Apostles model. Priests, religious, and laity would form one community. There would be no paid workers, but everyone would have his or her particular responsibility and contribution. Similarly, the minor seminary, diocesan headquarters, and houses of religious communities would follow this horizontal rather than vertical pattern of living.

This decentralization plan is part of the "village church" model emerging in Tanzania and other parts of Africa. This is a structural change in which the parish headquarters is no longer the focal point of the parish, but an administrative center and the center of communion and collaboration. The real Christian life and activities take place in the outstations and villages. In this plan priests, Sisters, and other pastoral workers spend much more time away from the parish headquarters; they regularly visit the outstations and villages to animate SCCs on the local level.

Bishop Mwoleka has identified five essential elements of a viable Christian community as demanded by the signs of the times:

1. All members of the community give themselves totally to God through their community. This self-surrender means being at the service, disposal, and mercy of the other members of the community.
2. The community comprises a cross section of the society that it is called to heal.
3. The different charisms, talents, and gifts of the members of the community are integrated in such a way that the members complement one another.
4. Like the first Christians, all the members of the community are of one heart and one mind; there is genuine consensus and unanimity.
5. The community lives not for itself but for others; it is sent to the world.

Models of decentralization are especially timely in an age that is questioning the validity of large institutions and cumbersome structures in the church. Large religious institutions can often "protect" their members from direct involvement with the poor and needy people. Person-to-person values can be lost in our activity and bureaucracy. Within their "religious environments" priests, Brothers, and Sisters can keep the laity at arm's length.

In Nyabihanga I found that the sharing experience of the first Christian communities was possible. We had a very unstructured lifestyle that could easily respond to the needs of others. In "a community with a human face" we could be flexible. Mealtimes and other community activities could always be changed to fit the weather, meetings, extra work. Unexpected guests were always welcome.

Trying to live for others and to put gospel values into action is demanding and challenging. Sharing community goods rather than owning them personally is an act of letting go. I discovered that sharing is at the heart of the Christian life and promotes mutual responsibility. Sensitivity to others takes on new meaning in a small, close-knit community, and makes one aware of how easy it is to project one's own felt needs onto others. The community, as I discovered, can be a great support for personal growth.

A key to this sort of community living is for the members to blend their various priorities and lifestyles. Genuine Christian community evolves through complementarity and interdependence. For the members to put up with each other's temperaments is important. When members of a community live beyond their own personal expectations, a depth of love and sharing develops.

While living in community with the Little Brothers in Nyabihanga I began to reflect more about the meaning of intimacy in the Christian life. The Little Brothers experience their vocation as a call to intimacy. Special dimensions are the daily hour of adoration before the Blessed Sacrament to deepen communion with the Lord, and the weekly "Review of Life," which is a period of close sharing in a spiritual setting. Here the Brothers touch the core and the spiritual depths of one another. They share intimate details of their lives, their loneliness, dryness in prayer, misunderstandings, difficulties in chastity. The other members of the community provide support and encouragement.

"Intimacy" is a word we have for a long time hesitated to use because of its many different meanings and associations. However, in contemporary spiritual literature "intimacy" is being used more and more to describe the core of Christian vocation. We are called to intimacy: first and foremost, intimacy with Christ, then intimacy with our brothers and sisters with whom we meet and share in so many situations of life. This growth in intimacy begins with oneself. We can know the power of God's life within us—the communion and indwelling of love. This love is revealed most deeply as it was enfleshed in Jesus; his being was called forth to the intimacy of total identification with humanity. The love of Jesus through the Spirit is poured forth in our hearts so that we are empowered to reach out and touch deeply the hearts and lives of our brothers and sisters.

To enter deeply into the life of another is a risk: one becomes vulnerable. Yet here—in a one-to-one relationship—is perhaps the greatest potential for personal growth. Sharing in the fullness of the humanity of another person can bring about liberation in one's own spirit. This frees one to love more, to be more receptive and open, and to give more of oneself. However, there is always the possibility that intimacy between two persons can become exclusive and close in on itself. This is part of the risk of loving. Genuine intimacy challenges the two persons to be open to the needs of others.

The experience of community life fosters intimacy on another level. Here the challenge is for each person to grow and develop within an atmosphere where good communication exists and where bonds of love can be forged. This requires self-giving with real generosity. In such an environment it is possible to grow together through the sharing of daily life and happenings, times and seasons of difficulty, joys and triumphs.

The experience of prayer can have a remarkable impact upon relationships between people, as well as on the growth of friendship and intimacy. To be able to share the mystical dimension with another is a profound experience. The practice of meditation can assist people in their search for friendship and intimacy. The detachment and empathetic knowledge that accompany the meditation process can help people to meet at the core of their beings and to love one another at a deeper level of awareness.

This deep intimacy nourishes and supports our ability to reach out to others. My own experience and the experience of others would seem to show that authentic intimacy faces outward. In all the dimensions of intimacy—intimacy with Christ, intimacy with another person, intimacy in community—we are called forth to be involved in the lives of other persons. We desire to share with others the deepest values of our own lives—values of love, peace, joy, commitment, service. Likewise, authentic intimacy awakens and stimulates a deep compassion for the pain and suffering of humankind. Whether as individuals or as community, we strive to touch our suffering brothers and sisters. René Voillaume, the founder of the Little Brothers, expresses this in a moving way: "The love we feel for God, the love we feel for Jesus Christ, must without question be accompanied either by contemplation or by a deep tenderness for men."

The ideal of authentic intimacy is the love and communion of the Father, Son, and Holy Spirit. Their intimacy reaches out in love for humankind. As we become more intimate with Jesus and with each other, we are called forth to share with other people. We become men and women for others.

Wasting Time with God

Every morning and evening the members of the bishop's community prayed together. Sometimes we used the psalms from the Swahili Breviary. At other times we conducted a Bible service or meditated in silence. There was something very special about praying together as a small community. It gave a certain quality and meaning to our lives that flowed into the rest of the day. Praying together seemed to unite us as brothers and sisters and to deepen our friendships, making it easier to work together in the kitchen, on the farm, and in our apostolic activities. We found the truth of this again and again in all our praying communities—in the Bible services of our SCCs, in the Sunday Eucharist, and in special recollection days of our outstation community. Participating in a praying community gave a real depth to our lives.

The importance of the praying community was revealed in the evaluation of a number of team-ministry experiments in Tanzania. These experiments involved priests who lived together and worked together. They covered three or four parishes as a team rather than working alone in separate parishes. When the team of priests prayed regularly together, a spirit of unity and cooperation was manifested in their apostolic work. But the teams that did not pray together on a regular basis began to divide up within two years. The work alone did not sustain the group. Without a praying community the zeal for team ministry dried up.

Often I shared in the one hour of silent adoration that the Little Brothers had every day in our chapel. This hour of quiet prayer (prayer of the heart or silent union prayer with Jesus) was a unique time of each day. It was a being prayer rather than a doing prayer. One person beautifully described it as "wasting time with God." Many years ago in the seminary a prayer-packed daily Holy Hour was held up as the ideal: meditation, Bible reading, a visit to the Blessed Sacrament, and the rosary were all crowded into sixty minutes. But it would seem that genuine spirituality is a prayerful life rather than the completing of a certain number of spiritual exercises every day. Our whole life should be a prayer.

I valued the quiet time I had in Nyabihanga. It taught me that in silence we can better establish ourselves in relation to God and to each other. Listening is a vital part of the contemplative experience, and as contemplation becomes a habit, the action (grace) of God transforms our hearts, attracting us to greater inward communion and propelling us outwardly to share this communion with others.

The contemplative person deliberately withdraws from the intense activity of daily life from time to time in order to explore and deepen fundamental human experience. For the contemplative it is this silent, seemingly empty element that makes his or her life truly a life of prayer.

For me it was a great discovery to find that touching fundamental human experience helps a person become more loving and compassionate toward others. If genuine prayer becomes an integral reality of the heart, all life and living will flow within this framework: love, communion, intimacy, growth, unselfishness. These qualities will enable us to reach out to the poor, the needy, the oppressed, to situations of injustice, turmoil, war. The praying person is of necessity as vulnerable as Jesus was on the cross, and must touch, embrace, and be identified with the anguish of humanity. As part of the prophetic call, we must stand within the cares and needs of all people and bring them before the face of God in prayer. Personal prayer neither can be sustained nor expanded in a vacuum. It is crucial that deep prayer be nourished by the concerns and cares, joy and happiness, pain and anguish of our world. As part of his prophetic mission, Jesus was involved with healing, touching, caring for those who needed his love—and the same must be true of us.

So that the reflective process may become integral to one's existence, it is important to be faithful to sustained prayer. This will lay a foundation for the time and seasons when one is called forth in ministry to tasks that might limit the actual time spent in praying. At each time one can fall back on the sustained, quiet intimacy one knows with the Lord—the prayer of the heart, which in the deepest sense is the presence of Jesus carried within.

More and more people are discovering that every Christian has a contemplative dimension in his or her life. To live the richness of the Christian life we regularly need time and space apart to touch the core of our being. In Nyabihanga I discovered that living with the people on the local level and having a regular time for quiet prayer were—each in its own way—a deep experience calling me back to my roots. This very rhythm of daily life in the village encouraged prayer and reflection. The slow pace of life created a contemplative mood and atmosphere for reflection and discernment. It was not just finding time for prayer; that I could find in Nairobi or New York. It was developing a being-approach and having enough quiet moments each day to sustain the flow. In this rural agricultural setting I discovered two special times of prayerful silence. The period around 6 A.M. was a time of awakening stillness. The night's calm still clung to the wet, shivering land, and prayer came easily. Slowly the silence of darkness turned into the expectancy of the first rays of the early morning sun and the busy farmwork ahead.

A second moment was the early evening—a time of gathering stillness. As the villagers returned to their homes and the joyful cries of children faded into the clusters of banana trees, a gentle calm descended on the land, like a soft, invisible rain. A hush permeated the village, and it was easy to pray.

Entering into the rhythm of Nyabihanga revealed an important dimension to our life of prayer: as individual Christians and as a faith community we tried to pray out of lived experience and into lived experience. The context of our prayer was the daily life of the village and our links with the parish, diocese, country, and rest of the world. We didn't try to leave the cares and concerns, problems and pain of our local situation at the door of the chapel. We placed the fullness of our human situation before the Lord. The African members of the bishop's community liked intercessory prayer best of all—to pray for our neighbors, our small communities, our village, our diocese, our nation. We placed before the Lord real concerns of our lives: our neighbor's sick child; the need for rain during the planting season; success of a lay-leadership seminar; a safe journey for the students returning to high school; peace on the border between Tanzania and Uganda. We tried to make sure that through service to others our prayer flowed into our daily life and work. For this reason during our Bible service we would plan concrete action to help the sick, poor, and needy people in our neighborhood and village. After interiorizing the gospel values in our own hearts, we then reached out to other people.

The person-centered values of the Washubi people helped me to discover another dimension of prayer and spirituality. One person put it this way: "Prayer is a child talking to his or her Father." Fundamentally, prayer is a loving relationship, an encounter with Jesus. In the Washubi society, where personal relationships are so important, the Christians quickly experienced Jesus as friend and brother. They liked a colloquy style of prayer where they could informally talk things over with Jesus.

The praying community can have important consequences for ministry. For many years the teaching catechumenate has been a major part of pastoral activity. The priest or catechist gathers together a group of people who are interested in learning about Christian doctrine. The religion teacher "teaches," that is, hands on the Deposit of Faith. Yet often this remains just an intellectual experience, touching the head but not the heart. Faith is a gift of God that touches a man or woman more deeply through heart values than through head values.

In Bukiriro outstation we began the "Praying and Serving Catechumenate." Bishop Mwoleka explained that the first step in the adult catechumenate is for the individual to pray every week for six months in his or her SCC. The catechumen does not learn the faith in a classroom but discovers the faith in a living faith community. This is an experience of God through the local praying community. The catechumen's newly discovered faith comes alive as the praying community moves from words to deeds, in concrete service to poor and needy people in the neighborhood. We found that this community experience of prayer leading to loving service touched peoples' hearts in a very deep way and transformed their lives.

My two years in Nyabihanga also helped me to understand in a deeper way the contemplative dimension of the missionary vocation. Our personal relationship with Jesus and his Spirit is the heart of all that we are and all that we do. Our missionary activity flows from our inner union with Jesus and his mission. This spiritual center is what gives meaning to our evangelizing, our reaching out to others, and our missionary presence.

Today when many people are searching for contemplative forms of missionary presence, different models of the missionary life that contain a contemplative dimension are emerging: (1) a team of missionaries living a life of community spiritual presence among the people; (2) an individual missionary living a life of spiritual presence as part of a community of local people; (3) missionaries living the contemplative dimension as part of their active ministry; for example, within a parish or team ministry context.

Many people ask: Can active missionaries integrate a contemplative dimension in their lives? Some say that this involves developing a contemplative attitude in an active lifestyle. Through experiencing God on a deeper level in our lives we can be carried by a consciousness of the Spirit throughout our whole day. A Trappist priest in Kenya offers this suggestion: to develop the contemplative dimension of one's life the busy missionary can spend twenty minutes in the morning and twenty minutes in the evening in contemplative prayer (quiet, affective prayer, not discursive mental prayer). These two periods can give a flow and harmony to the missionary's whole day.

This suggests that the real journey in life is the inner journey of the spirit. This is the longest and most important journey of our lives. It is a pilgrimage of the heart.

The Bishop's Seven-Year Dream

As Bishop Christopher Mwoleka traveled around Rulenge Diocese he saw that something vital was lacking in the Christian life of the people. A strong Christian tradition was missing. The people had few deep Christian convictions because of the strong practices of traditional religions, secret fears about witchcraft, and various social pressures. Religion had become a private affair. Christians lived their lives as individuals, not as a community. Genuine African Christianity was a long way from the everyday life of the people in the villages.

Bishop Christopher traveled and searched and pondered. He concluded that a plan of forming and deepening SCCs was needed to bring about a revolution and radical change in the church: "A new catechesis means, therefore, that we must make a resolve resolutely to get involved in the lives of one another," he said.

"The church must promote small Christian communities with a human face. . . . It has to be small enough to enable a network of interpersonal relationships to develop and grow among all the members. A sense of belonging must be fostered through services prompted by mutual concern."

To base the entire pastoral plan of Rulenge Diocese on SCCs was revolutionary in several ways. First, this method shifts church structures and attitudes away from the parish to the out-station and the SCC. The whole community becomes involved in catechesis and handing on the faith. Lay ministries can grow rapidly. Second, in the SCCs the local traditions and cultural values of the people can become impregnated with gospel values. Bishop Christopher states: "Providentially, the small Christian community, if developed on the right lines, will eventually replace the traditional African extended family or the clan. Just as baptism transforms a natural baby into the child of God, a small Christian community is nothing else but a baptized clan. The clan with all its culture, ethos, relationships, and institutions is not destroyed but purified and transformed." Third, SCCs provide the opportunity to transform the hearts and minds of people by enabling them to live a genuine Christian way of life in community. SCCs are moved by the power of Christ to move the world.

The actual establishing of SCCs throughout Rulenge Diocese began in 1976. Six people (two lay leaders, a catechist, a Sister, a priest, and Bishop Christopher) formed the diocesan training team. They conducted five-day seminars for all priests, religious, leaders of lay movements, and parish council leaders in each of the fifteen parishes. On Monday and Tuesday the team explained the main purpose of establishing SCCs, the way of grouping families together, and the manner of conducting the weekly Bible service. On Wednesday and Thursday the parish participants moved to an outstation for a similar seminar given to some two hundred representatives chosen from the surrounding villages. The Bible service was demonstrated not by the diocesan training team but by the parish training team.

On Friday the outstation (usually composed of several villages) was divided into fifteen to thirty communities, each consisting of about ten or twelve families. Two or three leaders who had been attending the seminar from the beginning had the responsibility of helping one small natural community get started. They visited each of the twelve families in the neighborhood group, moving from one family to another. They collected all the members from each family as they went along until everyone gathered together at the last house. There the lay people had their first meeting as a "small Christian community." They elected their prayer leader and participated in the Bible service as a distinct neighborhood community. They promised to meet once a week for a Bible service (on a weekday at a time fixed by them). The Bible service would take place at the home of a different family each week, every family taking its turn as host. After this first Bible service on Friday afternoon, all the small communities came together at a central place to participate in the Eucharist, which, celebrated with a real sense of spiritual renewal, marked the beginning of a new life of sharing in that outstation.

Through these seminars over three thousand SCCs were established in Rulenge Diocese. The heart of the small community is the weekly Bible service, which follows this general outline:

1. Opening song or prayer.
2. Short introduction to the liturgical theme.
3. Reading of the Gospel of the following Sunday (or another Scripture reading related to the liturgical season, marriage, thanksgiving, reconciliation, death, etc.).
4. Silent reflection.
5. Reading of the Gospel for the second time.
6. Sharing of reflections and thoughts on the Gospel.
7. Petitions (general intercessions).
8. Selection of some concrete practical action to be carried out during the following week.
9. Closing song or prayer.

These SCCs can be described in different ways: prayer groups with a social concern; schools of Christian love; families in the image of the communion of the Trinity; neighbors witnessing in their natural environment.

From the very first seminar Bishop Christopher and others realized that establishing SCCs was only the beginning. Rulenge Diocese needed a long-range plan to promote and animate the many SCCs. The first priority was to train lay leaders in each community. The bishop foresaw thirteen types of lay ministries (animators) in each SCC. He selected seven lay ministries for specialized training—one ministry per year. Bishop Christopher's dream became a "Seven-Year Plan to Train Leaders of the Small Christian Communities." This Seven-Year Leadership Training Program began in 1977 with the "Year of Prayer Leaders."

Instead of going to each parish the diocesan training team (now enlarged to ten to twelve members) conducted four six-day seminars in Rulenge town. Each parish sent a team of priests, Sisters, catechists, and lay leaders (men and women) to one of the seminars, which consisted of: (1) a special two-day retreat conducted by the bishop himself; spiritual formation and transformation of the Christian leaders themselves was the starting point and heart of the seminars; (2) two days of talks and explanation on the role and function of prayer leaders; (3) two days of practical experience and practical application.

Then the parish training teams conducted similar seminars in all the parishes and outstations until the prayer leaders of all the SCCs in the diocese had participated in a seminar. This seminar plan was repeated in 1978 ("Year of the Religious Formation Leader") and in 1979 ("Year of the Promoter of Self-reliance"). In 1980–83 seminars will be conducted for four other types of lay ministries: marriage counselors, promoters of community spirit, promoters of sacraments and spirituality, and coordinators.

Within the local Christian community, there is a sharing of responsibilities. Bishop Mwoleka sees the charisms of the different lay ministries, or animators, in this way:

1. A prayer leader animates the members of the community with the spirit of prayer, leads the weekly Bible service, and conducts Sunday services without a priest.
2. A religious formation leader aids the parents to fulfill their responsibilities toward their children and helps to form adult catechumens.
3. A promoter of self-reliance makes the members of the community aware of the financial needs of the church and promotes projects for fund-raising.

4. A marriage counselor befriends and helps couples before and after marriage.
5. A promoter of community spirit promotes brotherhood and concern for others and initiates projects for the common good.
6. An animator of sacraments and spirituality fosters the sacramental life of the community in various ways.
7. A coordinator sees to it that each charge is performed and that all are carried out in harmony.

Small Christian communities give the laity not only an opportunity to exercise responsibility in building a truly local church, but also provide a training ground for leadership.

In some dioceses of Tanzania lay leaders receive formal installation. This gives them public recognition and fosters permanence. In Rulenge Diocese we discussed the merits of this plan, but it was not adopted during my time there.

Besides the offices listed above, six other lay ministries are needed in the SCCs: youth counselor, song leader, communicator, cultural-affairs leader, social worker/health educator, and secretary.

The lay Christians have the main responsibility for the small communities on the local level. The role of priests, Brothers, and Sisters—both missionary and African—is not to take the initiative themselves, but to support the initiative of the lay leaders. Animation can take many forms—conducting lay leadership training programs, spiritual formation of lay Christians, and coordination and exchange of the activities and examples of the small communities. Through this process priests and religious can promote the development of lay ministries and a truly self-reliant, self-ministering, and self-propagating local church.

Stated another way, priests, Brothers, and Sisters (and even full-time lay pastoral workers) are "animators of the animators." They work with local lay leaders, who in turn work with the Christians in the individual SCCs.

What is new and different about this seven-year dream of Bishop Christopher? This can be answered in the context of Bukiriro outstation. The SCC plan produces a genuine decentralization in the church's structure—starting from the bottom rather than the top. Beginning in their own natural basic Christian communities, lay people have more responsibility and authority. Each of the eleven SCCs in Bukiriro has its own representative on the outstation council. Thus the people in each geographical section of Nyabihanga and Bukiriro villages have their own elected delegate. Each type of lay ministry operates in a similar way. After each SCC had elected its own religious-formation leader, the eleven leaders elected Severina Gwasa the leader/helper of the whole outstation. In turn, all outstation religious-formation leaders elected the leader for the subparish and parish levels on up to the person responsible for the whole diocese.

This new approach greatly increased the participation and zeal of the lay leaders. In the past the meetings of the Bukiriro Council had often to be postponed for lack of a quorum. But with the new system, over 80 percent of the representatives of the SCCs regularly attended the meetings held every two months.

Bishop Christopher developed a new terminology to go with the new plan of SCCs. Gradually the term "pastoral committee" has replaced the term "executive committee" on outstation, subparish, and parish levels. This emphasizes the fact that the local leaders are not administrators or executives but pastoral workers who serve the local community. During the Seven-Year Plan to Train Leaders of the Small Christian Communities, the work of SCCs, outstations, subparishes, and parishes is being placed increasingly in the hands of the pastoral committee. This committee consists of the seven leaders/helpers mentioned above, assisted by the catechist.

In the old structure the lay person in charge was the "chairperson" of the parish council. This conveyed an attitude of status or rank. The new designation is "coordinator/servant," to emphasize a service role in the context of shared ministries. The coordinators are servants in the pattern of Jesus Christ. They coordinate all the other ministries. The new names also explain the leaders' new roles. The treasurer of the pastoral committee is not just responsible for the money, but must promote self-reliance, a key dimension in the growth of the local church.

Gradually sacramental life in Bukiriro outstation has become more and more the responsibility of the SCCs and has been integrated into the local community's experiences. The first stage of the two-year adult catechumenate is a six-month period when the catechumen participates in the weekly activities of his or her SCC. Then the local leaders, such as the religious-formation leader and the promoter of sacraments and spirituality, instruct the catechumen, gradually initiating the person into the local faith community. Only at the end of the two-year period does the priest or catechist become involved.

The sacrament of baptism is an opportunity for SCC members to be fully involved. First, the religious-formation leader or the promoter of sacraments and spirituality consults members to determine if the parents of a child to be baptized are faithful members of the SCC and the outstation. Community members themselves conduct the investigation. The actual baptism takes place within a special Bible service of the child's (or adult's) own SCC in which members of the newly baptized person's community participate. In this way the new small community members and new Christians are welcomed into their neighborhood group, their village, and their outstation.

There is a similar plan for marriages. In October 1977 Andrea and Scholastica Ngenzi were married. Before the celebration all participated in the Bible service conducted by members of Mtakuja SCC. This was an opportunity to pray for the new couple and for the Christians of Mtakuja to welcome the bride (who came from a neighboring village) into their local community.

The sacrament of the sick, funerals, graveside prayer services, and blessings of pregnant mothers and newborn children are likewise carried out in the context of the SCCs.

A particularly delicate case occurs when second wives present their babies for baptism. Often the husbands are nonpracticing Catholics whereas the wives are active Catholics, except that they cannot receive the sacraments because of their improper marriages. First, the second wife's SCC discusses and evaluates her situation. Is she a faithful and conscientious member of the local community? If so, her child will be recommended for baptism to the Bukiriro Pastoral Committee. The committee will make its own evaluation and recommendation. Is the woman a faithful member of the outstation community? Often the deciding factor is not whether she participates in the Sunday Eucharist (important as this is), but if she is faithful in carrying out practical action in the community—helping needy people, performing Good Samaritan actions in her SCC, working on the church farm, and so forth. The key question is whether she lives her Christianity and is a good example of a "Christian in action" to her children and other Christians. If so, her child may be baptized.

Such cases as the foregoing, as well as other village and church matters, would be talked over in the evenings by our little group in Nyabihanga. If Bishop Christopher stayed over, he would join us, and often the conversation would turn to the growth of SCCs. The bishop explained that in lighting a wood fire one stick or log is not enough. To get a real fire going you need to put a number of sticks together, and then they help each other. So it is with the SCCs. A small group of people is better than one person. Then the fire of the Holy Spirit works in the group. If a parish or outstation has one or two small communities that are dynamic, these can stimulate growth. It is important that the core community remains alive and zealous so it can light others. As the Sukuma proverb says, "You never let the home fire go out."

As Bishop Christopher talked about community, his dreams went beyond his seven-year plan. He dreamed of integrated communities whose membership would cover a cross-section of society. Once he wrote:

The genuine Christian community we are talking about must find a place for every person who desires to join. A group of only males, or one of only females, cannot form a genuine community because in them you cannot find the necessary complementarity of charisms and talents. With them you cannot form a "natural environment," which everybody in society badly needs.

In the genuine Christian community we must find men and women, old and young, married and single, learned and simple, healthy and sick, professionals and the common, ordained and the lay. . . . Their lives, charisms, talents and shortcomings must be integrated to form a single whole, and function like an organism. So I dare to propose that the ideal Christian life for now and the future is a mixed community. A celibacy that needs to be protected by brick walls is completely out of place. There is a great need for celibacy in a mixed community.

During our evening conversations we posed such questions as "What was the first community?" and "What was the first Christian community?" After much discussion we finally agreed that the first community was the Trinity—Father, Son, and Holy Spirit. Their union and sharing is the heart of all community. Identifying the second community took a long time. We finally chose the good and bad angels and concluded that this community failed. We decided that the third community in history—Adam, Eve, Cain and Abel—failed too. The parents failed to live as an unselfish community and the children followed their bad example.

Passing over the whole range of communities in the Old Testament we came to the first Christian community—the Holy Family, Jesus, Mary, and Joseph. These three persons lived community values of unity, love, sharing, and service in such a special way that they are a perfect community model for families today. The next SCC was Jesus and his disciples. For them sharing together was a way of life. The Gospel narrates how this community was always reaching out to others in practical actions of love and mercy. The communities of the first Christians as described in the Acts of the Apostles were SCCs that challenge us to "go and do likewise" today.

One of Bishop Christopher's special gifts is his readiness to reevaluate and revise his pastoral plans. After four years (1976–79) how was his seven-year dream being realized? At first the cold facts are discouraging. Over three thousand SCCs have been started in Rulenge Diocese, but only about 15 percent are functioning well. The remaining 85 percent either collapsed, joined with stronger SCCs, or continue in a very limited way. Bishop Christopher does not regard this decline as irreversible. He believes that good seed has been planted, and in due time will show renewed life. To animate lay leaders in the outstations and the SCCs is the biggest need. The ongoing lay ministries training program is crucial and will produce lasting results, although slowly.

The bishop's dream of integrating all aspects of the pastoral work into the plan of SCCs is also a long-term process. Many years of education and formation of the Christians in Rulenge Diocese are needed. Rethinking all the sacraments in the context of small communities is a big challenge. Developing the role of the parish as a genuine communion of communities will take a long time.

A major criticism of the SCC plan in Rulenge is that the general strategy has been planned and carried out by the authorities from the top, the directive approach. The initiative and structure have come from the bishop, the priests, and a few lay leaders. This is in contrast to a conscientization approach, which first helps the local people to become aware of their own needs and problems. If this were done, a structure would gradually emerge from the needs of the people, rather than being imposed from the top.

However, it would seem that in many cases a certain structure and plan are needed to start the SCC process, especially when local lay leaders must be trained. After the foundations have been built, and the communities have a permanent quality, the time will be ripe for the conscientization process. This will be especially effective in treating crucial areas such as lack of Christian traditions, witchcraft, deeply rooted social and cultural pressures, and economic development. It is to be hoped that continuing animation from the top and emerging felt needs from the bottom will work together.

The Ups and Downs of Nyabuliga

Three Bernadette Sisters lived in the Nyabuliga section of Nyabihanga from January 1974 to February 1976. To encourage the Christians to pray together, they started a weekly Gospel Sharing Group (the forerunner of the weekly Bible service of the SCC). A small dedicated group of Christians, mainly women, prayed and reflected with the Sisters. However, when the Sisters left in February 1976, the Christians of Nyabuliga postponed the prayer meeting for a week, saying that they had a lot of work in the fields. The week stretched to two weeks, to a month, to two months. When the Little Brothers and I arrived in early September 1976, the Nyabuliga Christians had not met once since the Sisters left. Clearly it was the presence and encouragement of the Sisters that had kept the Gospel Sharing Group alive. We asked ourselves: How can we break through this classic pattern wherein prayer groups are successful when priests, religious, or zealous catechists are conscientious animators but tend to dissolve after a period of time when they are on their own?

We tried to break this pattern during the four-day seminar in November 1976 that introduced the whole plan and practice of SCCs to Bukiriro outstation. The seminar team tried to form natural neighborhood communities based on the ten-family cells of the government. The basic plan of the Tanzania Catholic Bishops Conference to form an SCC with from five to twelve families was unrealistic for Nyabuliga. In many families of the immediate area the parents belonged to African traditional religions and only the children were Catholic. In other families there were "nonpracticing Catholics," persons who were baptized at birth when in danger of death, but who never practiced their faith afterward; or "occasionally practicing Catholics," persons who attended the Sunday Eucharist only on big feasts. The result was that the Nyabuliga SCC started with twenty-three families, an unusually large number of families for a neighborhood group.

The membership of the Nyabuliga SCC was typical in many respects and revealed the pastoral challenge in Nyabihanga and Bukiriro. In the twenty-three families there was not one man who could receive the sacraments. Every man had either a second wife or had not yet married in church. Following a strong Washubi custom, Angelo Bulantondera, the elected prayer leader, had recently taken a second wife. A few women (all first wives) could receive the sacraments, but not one woman regularly attended the Sunday Eucharist at Bukiriro outstation, which was just over a mile away. The young people, especially the schoolboys, were the most faithful and active members.

To add to our problems, the majority of the adults could not read or write. The fact that he was illiterate hindered Angelo's growth as a leader. To learn about the Bible and the plan of SCCs was a slow process, and Angelo needed several months to memorize the steps of the Bible service. If the schoolboys were missing, there was often no one to read the Gospel in Shubi.

On the other hand, Nyabuliga SCC was not typical because the Little Brothers and I were members. The Christians often depended on us to take the initiative and make decisions. At times we had purposely to stay in the background so the lay leaders could develop experience and confidence. For example, we would refuse to read the Gospel in Swahili if someone else could do it. Another worry was that the local Christians were participating just to please us.

In the beginning the seminar team and the local leaders visited each family in the Nyabuliga SCC to explain the meaning and activities of the new neighborhood group. The villagers—Christians and others—responded enthusiastically. Many attended the weekly Bible service and performed the practical action during the first weeks. Then in January 1977, Thomas told me, "Without a priest our small Christian community is very weak." He went on to explain that without my animation work and the supportive presence of the two Little Brothers, the small community would break up within a month.

I didn't want to believe this, but slowly I came to realize that I had been helping the Nyabuliga SCC too much, and the Christians were not developing personal responsibility and self-reliance. I then began visiting other SCCs, leaving Nyabuliga more and more on its own.

Then occurred a whole series of up and downs, which I found hard to understand. Some community members faithfully attended the Bible service, but were "busy" during the practical action (such as fetching water and firewood for a sick woman). Others participated in the Bible service in their neighborhood, but didn't have time to walk to Bukiriro on Sunday for the Eucharist. Local customs often won out over church activities. Several men attended the Christmas liturgy at the outstation. When the annual celebration of Nyabihanga village occurred on the same Sunday that a newly ordained priest was celebrating one of his first masses at Bukiriro outstation, only four adults from the whole village attended the Eucharist.

These examples showed me how fragile the Christianity in Nyabuliga was. The Christians would participate to a point, but a sudden event—rain, a birth, a visitor, a big feast, even the death of Angelo's goat—was always an excuse not to get involved. As one of the Christian leaders said, Christianity was not a deeply rooted value in the lives of the people. Gospel values had not penetrated the hearts of the villagers.

Yet through the total pastoral plan of building and making permanent SCCs we hoped that Bishop Christopher's "revolution" would occur. As the SCC process evolved we tried to learn its strengths and weaknesses, and we kept complete records to evaluate each community's successes and failures.

The main responsibilities of the members of the Nyabuliga SCC are to participate in the weekly Bible service on Thursday afternoon and do the weekly practical action. During the first complete year (52 weeks) there were: forty-nine Bible services; three weeks without a Bible service, the reasons being: national holiday in Tanzania (week 5), heavy rain (week 13), the woman— a second wife—at whose home we were supposed to have the service had just been sent away by her husband (week 38). During the three weeks in which there was no service, our prayer leader, Angelo, did not make an effort to change the day from Thursday to later in the week.

A statistical analysis of the forty-nine services reveals the following averages per service:

22.8 persons in attendance per service (5.0 men; 7.2 women; 10.6 young people and children)
 1.9 Reflections on the Gospel presented by the members per service
 6.6 prayers of petition offered by the members per service

The following comments can be made:

1. These figures are "inflated" and give a better picture than the reality. Since the Little Brothers, various visitors, and I regularly attended the weekly Bible service this added two, three, or four persons to the weekly averages of attendance. From the Nyabuliga SCC itself only two or three men normally attended. Regularly, villagers who were just passing by would attend the service without any real commitment. For a number of women it was a social occasion, when they could meet and talk with other women from their section of the village—either before or after the service.

2. Aside from priests and Brothers, only four people consistently attended: Angelo Bulatondera and the three schoolboys—Thomas, Christopher and John.

3. Many Christians attended the service when it took place near their home. They would not attend when it involved walking a distance of five or ten minutes.

At the end of each Bible service the members of the Nyabuliga SCC decided on some practical action for the following week. During the first complete year there were forty-three weeks when some practical action was accomplished:

> *27 times:* working on the small farm of the Nyabuliga SCC, which included cultivating, planting beans and corn, weeding, harvesting, and preparing the beans and corn for sale
>
> *10 times:* taking water, firewood, and food to a sick person or a mother whose child had died
>
> *9 times:* taking up a collection—usually thirty to forty-five cents—for a sick person or for a mother whose child had died (on one occasion the collection was a gift of $3.90 for a newly ordained priest in the parish)
>
> *3 times:* cleaning the church or the grounds around the church or the place for the eucharist
>
> *2 times:* cultivating the field of a neighbor who had had a recent death in the family
>
> *1 time:* contributing three pounds of beans for the harvest collection of Bukiriro outstation
>
> *1 time:* cooking a meal for a group of visiting catechists

From this account the following conclusions can be drawn: the overall plan of SCCs stresses helping the poor, sick, and other needy persons, that is, works of mercy. These practical actions were the best sign of the Christian spirit and dedication of the members of the Nyabuliga SCC. However, only a small number of Christians were faithful in carrying out these kinds of Good Samaritan works. Often they refused to help needy people in the village either because these people were not Christians or because they had not joined the SCC.

The farm plot of the Nyabuliga SCC was its most successful

project, and the best-cultivated field of all the communities in the outstation. After the harvest the beans were sold for $17.10 and the corn for $6.30. Half the money was put into the treasury of the outstation, and half into the treasury of the Nyabuliga SCC.

To many this may seem a small amount of money, but for a relatively poor area such as Ngara District where self-reliance in church matters is still a new idea, this profit represents real success. As a basis of comparison, the *zaka* (annual church tax) in Bukiriro outstation is seventy cents for men and fifty cents for women, whereas in other parts of Tanzania it is often two or three dollars.

A big problem occurred when the Christians had to decide how to use the $11.70 in the Nyabuliga treasury. Almost everybody said that it should be used for a beer party. They felt that they had done the work on the small farm, and so they should "get something for their efforts." They didn't see why the money should be used to help the poor and the sick. It was finally decided that half the money would be used for a beer party, and half for special needs of the SCC, such as a notebook and pen for the community secretary and a gift for the catechist.

Some of the loyal Christian women in the Nyabuliga SCC had husbands who belonged to African traditional religions; they did not understand the purpose of the SCC farm. On one occasion, when we wanted to use part of the profits of the Nyabuliga community farm as a gift for the retiring catechist Salvatori, one of the non-Christian husbands objected. He used a Shubi proverb: "A hoe does not leave its field," meaning that the profits from the farming should be used by the people who actually do the work and not for outside purposes. Educating both the members and the nonmembers to the purpose of the SCC and the importance of concrete acts of love and service was indeed difficult.

During the second year (mid-November 1977 to mid-November 1978) the attendance pattern was similar. There were fifty Bible services and forty-four weeks of practical action, revealing a consistency in the action of the Christian community. Then, in December 1978, the Christians took the initiative. Realizing that a single SCC was too large and unwieldly, spread over a wide area as it was, they divided into three smaller communities— Nyabuliga A, Nyabuliga B, and Nyabuliga C. This was a significant step and worked well, especially with the Bernadette Sisters animating the three communities from time to time.

Starting an SCC can be compared to a mother teaching a child how to walk. A new SCC needs help to stand on its own feet. It tries to stand up; it falls down; it gets help; it tries again. Eventually it stands on its own. And, with a little more help, the SCC finally walks on its own.

Helping a weak or ailing SCC is like giving a blood transfusion to a patient. For a period the SCC, like the patient, needs help and strength from the outside. But after building up its strength, the SCC can finally continue on its own. After much trial and error Nyabuliga SCC can now stand and walk on its own. From time to time it needs animation and help from the outside, but it is slowly developing responsibility and self-reliance.

The ups and downs of Nyabuliga highlight the challenge of developing permanent SCCs. Nyabuliga illustrates the classic reasons for the failure of SCCs in Rulenge Diocese and elsewhere in East Africa: the Christians lack a deep faith (as one pastoral worker put it, "The members of the SCCs do not have Christian hearts and Christian convictions"); genuine Christian foundations and traditions are missing; many Christians do not understand the purpose and plan of the SCCs; and there are very few dedicated, creative leaders.

Yet through the help of the Holy Spirit and everyday experience a process of growth and self-identity is gradually taking place. In the beginning, needy people in Nyabihanga would come to the Little Brothers, the Bernadette Sisters, or me for clothes. After it was explained that helping the needy is the responsibility of the whole local community, Angelo, our prayer leader, would present all the community needs during the discussion part of our weekly Bible service. The members then decided which people needed help the most. The gift of clothes or other kinds of help became the joint decision and responsibility of the whole SCC.

Let the Small Communities Speak

Although the members of the Nyabuliga SCC were faithful in attending the weekly Bible service on Thursday afternoon, during our first full year Angelo and the three schoolboys—Thomas, Christopher, and John—were the only Christians who ever gave a reflection or a short explanation after the reading of the Gospel. Occasionally Angelo would say: "I don't understand this Gospel. I ask Father Joseph to help us." So I—or one of the Little Brothers—would give a short explanation.

I asked myself: Why were the women always silent? Why was it so hard for the Christians to participate in the gospel reflection part of the Bible service? We finally discovered that we were starting the wrong way. We started with Scripture rather than life. We always used the gospel of the following Sunday. But most of the Christians, including almost all the adults, could not read or write. They weren't familiar with the New Testament; often it was new and strange to them. Many times they didn't understand the meaning of the gospel passages.

Added to this problem were various cultural traditions of the Washubi people. The women were not used to speaking in front of a mixed group of men and women. The schoolchildren were reluctant to speak in front of their elders. The result was silence.

For a long time the importance of a life-centered catechesis, which begins with the daily life of the people on the local level, had been considered. The starting point for discussion must be the life of the people, a concrete event or situation, a slice of life, not Scripture or doctrine. Then we could ask, "What light does the Gospel bring to this situation we are discussing?"

When this life-situation approach was first tried, Christopher, the prayer leader for that day, asked the Christians to begin by mentioning the "happenings" of the previous week—events that had taken place in our SCC, in Nyabihanga village, and in Bukiriro outstation since our last Bible service. Petro, one of the oldest men, immediately mentioned the death of Emmanuel's child. Two different women, Margaret and Anastasia, referred to the slide show that had been presented in the village two days earlier. Athanasius remarked that many men had come to the Bible service that day. Another man mentioned the problem of witchcraft in our village.

The silence was broken. The SCC was speaking. The women gave comments for the first time. It was all so simple. When the starting point was a life situation, the people immediately entered into the discussion. Everyone, no matter how little educated, was capable of and interested in discussing his or her own life.

After these "happenings" had been mentioned, Christopher chose one example—the death of Emmanuel's child—for further discussion and reflection. Emmanuel was a faithful member of our SCC and we all shared in his deep sorrow. We discussed the Christian meaning of death, and Christopher read from Matthew 14 about the death of John the Baptist. The reflections that followed the gospel reading focused on death and resurrection— how John the Baptist, Emmanuel's child, and all of us share in Christ's Paschal Mystery.

This life-situation approach to the weekly Bible service opened a new door for all our SCCs. The Christians participated much more when the service began with the happenings of their lives. They enjoyed "searching the Scriptures." The gospel passage that was selected spoke to their concrete situation and their questions at that time. This life-centered approach helped them to integrate gospel values into their African culture.

Besides starting the weekly Bible service from life situations of the people, we experimented with using African proverbs. We would start with a proverb and then move into a related Scripture passage. The African people love proverbs, and the Christians were eager to explain and discuss various proverbs and to find relevant Bible passages. On one occasion, in reflecting about the values of unity and community, we used the proverb "You cannot play the drum with one finger." The Washubi version of this proverb is, "One finger cannot kill a louse." In discussing the meaning of this proverb, the Christians emphasized the importance of sharing, working together, and supporting one another in the family, neighborhood, village, and outstation. This helped them to reflect on the importance of their SCCs. The Bible passages chosen were Jesus sharing with his disciples before ascending to heaven (Luke 24 and John 21) and the descriptions of the first Christian communities of believers (Acts of the Apostles 2 and 4).

Other popular proverbs were:

1. "Blood is thicker than water." The discussion here centered on personal relationships and the close bonds in the family and the clan. One man mentioned the African custom of two close friends cutting their arms and putting a small amount of their

blood in a pot of beer. The beer is then drunk to symbolize that their close friendship is like a blood relationship. For the Bible text we used 1 Corinthians 11:23–26 to explain that Jesus Christ invites us to drink his blood in the Eucharist in order to share his life. Our bond with Jesus and with each other in the Eucharist is the closest relationship we have; it is our deepest blood relationship.

2. "Education is an ocean." The Christians explained that education does not end: we can always keep on learning. The discussion led to the conclusion that love is like an ocean; it has no end. Christ calls us to love everyone and at all times. For the Bible text we chose 1 Corinthians 13:1–13, on the primacy of love.

3. "To dig is weariness; to reap is joy." The Washubi often use this proverb; indeed, they live its meaning in their everyday lives. In the farming cycle the first part is hard work: to clear the land, to cultivate the soil, to plant the seed, to weed the beans or corn. But the last part is easy: to harvest the crop and finally to eat it. A similar proverb is "He who earns his living in the sun, eats in the shade." Gospel passages used for these proverbs were the Parable of the Sower (Matthew 13 and Mark 4) and the Parable of the Weeds (Matthew 13).

Another way of using proverbs can be illustrated by "When elephants fight, the grass gets hurt," expressing the feeling of powerlessness in the midst of larger forces. When local government leaders quarrel and oppose each other, the simple villagers suffer. A related proverb is "That which eats you up is your clothes [or the thing nearest to you]." Village leaders can manipulate and exploit the local people in the name of government policy or ethnic group customs. Various practices in the local community itself, such as witchcraft and the invocation of evil spirits, oppress the people.

We found the use of proverbs very helpful as part of the conscientization process: to help the village people on the local level to reflect on their situation, and to discuss and analyze the different forces at work in their communities. A deeper awareness of their local problems led to concrete action in bettering their lives.

"Proverb evangelization" and "proverb catechesis" have been effective in other parts of Tanzania as well as our own. A priest working with the Wasukuma makes effective use of a very typical

Sukuma proverb: "To marry off your son is to swallow a stone." To swallow a stone is, of course, to do something hard. Cows are very important to the Wasukuma herders and are used for the marriage bride-wealth. For a Sukuma father to give many cows as the bride-wealth for his son's marriage is a big sacrifice and difficult, even though he is proud that his son is taking a wife. From the Scriptures a parallel experience might be Mark 8:34, where Jesus says, "If anyone wants to be a follower of mine, let him renounce himself and take up his cross and follow me." To be a disciple of Jesus means denying oneself and making sacrifices—in effect, to do something difficult, such as swallowing a stone.

In all these examples the life of the local people (as reflected in the African proverbs) is studied in the light of the gospel. The approach is from life to faith. Life and religion are linked, not separated. The Good News is integrated into the environment and life situation of the people. For the SCC this is a creative and formative experience. It is the local faith-community's experience of God's activity in history, the recognition of the Spirit of Jesus at work in the lives of his people.

A third way in which we might start the weekly Bible service was to use a common saying or idiomatic expression such as "Unity is strength" or "A promise is a debt." We followed the same steps as when using a proverb, and again the Christians spontaneously entered into the discussion and reflections.

Using a short drama or humorous play was also very popular. The Christians would dramatize an event (for example, a marriage problem), a value (for example, self-reliance), or a gospel story. The Cure of the Blind Man and the Parable of the Good Samaritan were especially popular. SCC members would enthusiastically discuss the meaning of the play and apply it to their everyday lives.

In addition to the weekly Bible services, the life-situation approach could be used in Sunday and weekday homilies. In this environmental preaching of the Word of God, the members of the congregation were asked to mention events from the past week. The Christians would usually give four or five examples, such as a recent wedding in the outstation; carrying trees, sand, and stones to enlarge the church; a catechists' seminar; harvesting the beans on the church farm; the death of one of the Christians; a big celebration to mark Independence Day in Tanzania. Then the Liturgy of the Word, especially the Gospel, would be related to these examples.

The "peak moments" in the lives of the people (birth, adulthood, marriage, reconcilation, death, and so forth) were ideal occasions to use a life-centered catechesis to integrate the gospel message with the African cultural experience. The "grain of wheat" analogy (John 12:24) was helpful in explaining the meaning of baptism. The Shubi farmers know very well that they have to bury their bean or corn seeds in the ground before they can bear new life. So they could existentially relate to the sacrament of baptism, when people have to die to the sinfulness of their past lives before they could rise up to a new life in Christ.

Sometimes a member of the congregation would explain a certain proverb during the Sunday homily. The many African proverbs on unity and community were helpful in emphasizing the importance of our SCCs. Applications to daily life came easily. They didn't have to be solemn or pedantic. During the month that the Christians were asked to carry water to make mud bricks to enlarge the church, to get volunteers was a real struggle; but when they were reminded of the proverb "To dig is weariness; to reap is joy" they laughingly agreed that "To fetch water is weariness, but to have a large church is joy."

Presenting and transmitting the Christian message through African thought patterns, oral traditions, and life situations is an obvious method of evangelization, but we were slow in beginning to use it. Pope Paul VI reminded us of this in his apostolic exhortation *On Evangelization in the Modern World*:

> Evangelization loses much of its force and effectiveness if it does not take into consideration the actual people to whom it is addressed, if it does not use their language, their signs and symbols, if it does not answer the questions they ask, and if it does not have an impact on their concrete life.

Yet there must be something more. It is not just a matter of translating and adapting the Christian message into the language and symbols of the African people. The Good News of Jesus Christ is communicated through the experience of the African people themselves within their local environment. God's self-revelation through people in history makes the African people (like people everywhere) a Fifth Gospel.

This puts the SCCs' experience of "searching the Scriptures" in a new light. The local Christians read and reflect on Scripture as God's living Word to find a description and narration of what they are actually living and experiencing. They do not merely seek a justification and legitimization of their actions, in the sense that an outside authority, such as the Bible, proves a certain conclusion. Jesus Christ's Good News of salvation can be both an affirmation and a challenge to the local community's experience. This is a dynamic two-way process. In reflecting on their life the SCC (a Fifth Gospel) goes to God's revelation in the four Gospels. In turn, the four Gospels throw light on present revelation (the SCC as a Fifth Gospel).

It is difficult to understand why both local priests and missionary priests in Africa have been so slow to respond to this new approach. Part of the reason may be that we have followed a limited theology of revelation. This theology sees revelation primarily as a set of doctrines to be proclaimed and "handed over." Intellectual assent is called for, and too often Christians become consumers of religion. A missionary in Upper Volta pointed out: "Experience shows that it is by starting off from these 'organized wholes' (doctrine or ecclesial realities) that our church is still living on Western culture and theology. . . . It is no longer possible to start off from some 'pre-established framework,' insofar as this framework is culturally determined from the outside."

The contemporary theology of revelation emphasizes the communication of God himself to his people. Revelation is an ongoing, dynamic process of God's self-disclosing presence, which changes persons' hearts as well as their minds, transforming their whole way of life. Revelation takes place in history, in the everyday events of the lives of individuals and communities. It is not primarily conceptual or verbal, but an experience of God's presence at the heart of everyday living.

The pastoral implication of this contemporary theology of revelation is that evangelization must deal seriously with the life of the people to be evangelized. To take the example of Africa: the starting point of evangelization is the life of the African people—

the underlying values and ideals that give meaning to their lives. Through the concrete events of their lives God is calling the African people to open themselves to his saving grace. The Spirit of God is truly among them.

From my experience in Tanzania I am convinced that missionary activity should be geared much more to establishing SCCs in which people discuss and reflect upon their lives and the lives of their neighbors and respond to the revelation taking place. In this way the local people themselves develop an authentic expression of their faith, instead of receiving the forms and expressions that have grown out of the historical experience of people of a different time and place.

In this whole process the entire Christian community is responsible for evangelization and catechesis. Each person has a contribution to make to the evangelization of the whole community. As Saint Paul says in 1 Corinthians 12:4: "To each person the manifestation of the Spirit is given for the common good." The SCCs themselves provide a unique opportunity for the development of different gifts and ministries. Through these groups laymen and laywomen exercise real responsibility in building a truly local church and developing an expression of their faith from within their own cultural experience.

$6.45 Saves a Life

Melia was mentally sick. During the national celebrations on July 7 she drank a lot of locally made alcohol which slowly began to affect her brain. About thirty-five years old, of medium height and graceful mien, Melia was an attractive woman until she began to neglect her physical appearance. She stopped eating; she refused to take care of her children; her customary smile disappeared. Once a faithful Christian, she stopped participating in the Sunday Eucharist. Her devoted husband, Alfaxon, grew worried.

August and September passed. By October Melia was much worse. She had become very thin, and threw on the ground any food given to her. When delirious, she tried to put her hand in a fire or purposely cut herself on sharp rocks. Ugly, open wounds covered her legs and feet. In a daze she wandered naked through Nyabihanga village. At night she slept in the nearby forest.

Naturally Alfaxon and his neighbors were very concerned. None of the local medicine was of any avail. At night Alfaxon had to tie up his wife to prevent her from wandering outside and hurting herself. Melia went from bad to worse. Her open wounds became infected. She would mumble incoherently or laugh hysterically. The villagers said that she was crazy and would soon die.

About this time we had an SCC seminar in Bukiriro. The Christians were very concerned about Melia and decided to help her. If she were to be saved, she would have to go to the hospital immediately. The chairperson of Nyabihanga village wrote a letter to the government leader in Rulenge requesting a car to take Melia to Murgwanza Hospital about forty-five miles away. One of the cell leaders rode his bicycle to Rulenge to deliver the letter in person.

Meanwhile all the SCCs of Nyabihanga worked together to help Melia. A special collection was taken at the weekly Bible services—two pennies, a nickel, a dime. The people were very poor, but many contributed. The total was $6.45—little by Western standards, but a large amount for a Tanzanian village that was not used to such collections. The money was given to Alfaxon for food and other necessities at the hospital. In the meantime the Christian community helped Melia in many ways. Some brought water and firewood; others brought food for her children.

The letter written by the village chairperson did not go unheeded. On Saturday afternoon a government Land-Rover arrived to take Melia to the Murgwanza hospital. Alfaxon and his oldest daughter accompanied Melia, who had to be tied down so that she wouldn't jump out of the car.

Two weeks later Alfaxon returned to report that Melia had received medicine at the hospital and was quieter. The SCCs continued to help, especially during the weekly practical action. The bishop's community gave powdered milk and sugar for Melia's youngest children. Some Christians helped Alfaxon to plant beans on his small farm and to weed his banana plantation. Here was the real meaning of Christian community—love and service in action.

During the next few months we heard that Melia was slowly

recovering. Her mind had begun functioning normally again. Her raw wounds had begun to heal. Her life had been saved.

Finally, in April 1977, Melia returned to Nyabihanga almost completely recovered. She felt depressed from time to time, and one sore on her leg still hadn't healed completely; but she was smiling for the first time in over eight months. She began caring for her children, and even attended the weekly Bible service. As one of our neighbors said, "The members of the small Christian communities saved her life."

Melia's story points out the real foci of the SCCs: loving the poor, helping the needy, reaching out to others. At the heart of the Christian life are Jesus' words: "I give you a new commandment: love one another; just as I have loved you, you also must love one another. By this love you have for one another, everyone will know that you are my disciples" (John 13:34–35).

Many times during the SCC seminars and discussions we returned to this basic truth: to follow Jesus is not just to pray or think nice thoughts, but to perform deeds of love and mercy. We stressed that all the weekly Bible services should have a practical-action dimension—specific acts of mercy and service—flowing out of the community prayer and reflection. Often Bishop Christopher emphasized the need to drive out selfishness and individualism in our lives because "Christianity is living for others."

After many evaluations of our SCCs we concluded: prayer is important, but the weekly Bible services alone can slowly lose their dynamism; community is important, but togetherness by itself can become stagnant. The surest sign of a successful and dynamic SCC is its faithfulness to the weekly practical action—reaching out to the poor and the needy. Through this outreach the SCC develops a meaning, an identity, a focus. Invariably, through the practical-action dimension, Christians intensify their involvement and commitment. They begin a deeper life of sharing and service.

This was especially true of Mtakuja SCC, the most effective SCC in Bukiriro outstation and the community of our catechist, Astheria Ngenzi. The Christians in Mtakuja had a very special spirit and dedication. During the first year they had a perfect record of attendance at the Bible service. Even more important, they carried out their practical action every week except one, and on that one week they failed to do the proposed action because it rained. This single failure made them seem human, and thus a believable model for others to follow.

I remember participating in a Bible service of Mtakuja SCC in September 1977. During the discussion on possible practical actions, one member mentioned the plight of a poor widow in the area. She was not a Christian. She lived alone in a miserable little house she had put up herself. The Mtakuja Christians decided to build a new house for this widow. The following Saturday afternoon about twenty Christians from Mtakuja and the neighboring Kukamasale SCC worked together. They dug holes for the foundations, brought poles for the structure, and grass for the walls and roof. In a few hours the new thatched-roof house was finished and the grateful widow moved in before the October rains.

Dedication to practical action on a weekly basis was not easy. Sometimes the Christians would refuse to help others; they would give all kinds of excuses, such as lack of time, sickness in the family, bad weather, a long distance to travel. At one Bible service of the Nyabihanga SCC we discussed ways of helping Angelo, whose daughter Donata was very sick. One member suggested taking a collection, but others argued that this was not necessary. Nobody contributed any money. There was silence in the prayer group. Finally Bukobwa, an elderly man who was not a Christian, took out a shilling (about 15 cents) and gave it to Angelo, saying, "This can help." By this spontaneous gesture Bukobwa had evangelized us Christians.

In animating the SCCs we used many ways of emphasizing the practical-action dimension of the weekly Bible service. One Tuesday afternoon I attended the weekly service at the home of Theresa, one of the most faithful Christians in Bukiriro village. Following the African custom she prepared a place for us to pray together outdoors. She arranged straw mats in a circle with fresh flowers in a vase in the center. But Theresa was embarrassed to put her old plastic crucifix next to the flowers. The crucifix had no arms. It had probably been brought to Tanzania by a missionary many years before, and had passed around several families. I said to Theresa, "Don't worry, Theresa. This crucifix is fine. I'm sure it has a special meaning for us."

After one of the leaders had read the Lenten Gospel, there was a period of silence followed by shared reflections. Suddenly it dawned on me what that old, battered, armless crucifix was saying to this group of fifteen Christians praying together. Jesus Christ was asking us to be his arms and to reach out to the poor, the needy, the sick, the suffering, the oppressed. To this thought the Christians responded immediately. During the last part of the Bible service we decided to help Anna, one of our neighbors who had two sick children. We gathered firewood and fetched water for the mother while she stayed at home with her children.

There were two Bible passages that we often used in our seminars. One was the teaching of Saint James that faith is dead without works:

> Take the case, my brothers, of someone who has never done a single good act but claims that he has faith. Will that faith save him? If one of the brothers or one of the sisters is in need of clothes and has not enough food to live on, and one of you says to them, "I wish you well; keep yourself warm and eat plenty," without giving them these bare necessities of life, then what good is that? Faith is like that: if good works do not go with it, it is quite dead (James 2:14–17).

These words were the basis of one of our favorite sayings in the outstation: "Words without actions are useless."

The other often-used passage was the Parable of the Good Samaritan (Luke 19:29–37), which we applied again and again to our lives in Bukiriro and Nyabihanga. In this parable we could see what Christianity in action ought to be. The Christians searched out ways that as individuals and as a community they could be "good Washubi." They came to realize that our neighbor is not only the person who meets us on our way, the person who comes to us for help, whom we help on our terms, in our style, out of our own security and abundance. Our neighbors are also the persons whom we meet on their path, on their terms. Here our love and service is a real reaching out beyond our own control and expectation. This parable challenges us to be "neighbor" to the person outside our community, our village, our ethnic group, our value system. In this experience it is we who are evangelized and changed.

Continuous reflection on the importance of practical action—especially helping the poor and needy—led me to another conclusion: helping the needy while living in a small community "with a human face" is relatively easy; in our village people responded spontaneously to needy persons. But when living or working in a larger community or institutional setting—large religious house, school, large apartment house, office building—it is much more difficult to help. We can miss the human face in the crowd. Or the human face may be blurred. Or there may be too many human faces all at once. And yet the same challenge for genuine practical action is there.

The Inspiration of Astheria

On the Friday before Christmas 1977, we had a day of prayer and recollection at Bukiriro outstation. About fifty Christians participated in the two talks, silent reflection, Penitential Service, and Eucharist. After the Eucharist at about 4 P.M., I joined some of the lay leaders at Salvatori's home for a traditional meal of beans and bananas. Our new catechist, Astheria Ngenzi, was missing, so I asked Petro Gwanka where she was. Petro told me that Astheria would come later.

Near the end of the meal Astheria arrived carrying her hoe. She told me that the Christians of the Mtakuja SCC had decided to clean and smooth the grounds around our simple church as part of their weekly practical action. They worked immediately after the end of recollection day, so Astheria worked alongside the other Christians until everything was finished.

Through similar examples of service and sharing, Astheria was a constant inspiration to me and the other Christians. She was truly a person for others. I remember her walking miles in the scorching sun to visit a sick woman or teach religion in the grade school. I remember her arriving soaking wet at the bishop's house in Nyabihanga, saying, "Even though it rained I didn't want to miss Mass today." I remember her walking nine miles to Rulenge to attend an SCC seminar. I remember her volunteering to carry buckets of water from the river to the church to make bricks—walking barefoot up the steep hill with a heavy bucket on her head. I remember her patiently teaching the young children the meaning of the sacraments. She was always the first to come and the last to leave.

We worked very closely together, and I grew to admire and love her many qualities and gifts, especially her total availability and service to others. I marvel at God's hand in Astheria's life, because most of these gifts and qualities could have remained hidden. But they came to light. This is her story.

Astheria was a bright child and did well in the Bukiriro grade school. As is the case with many intelligent children in mediocre schools in rural Tanzania, she failed the high school entrance exam, so after finishing eighth grade in 1969 she returned home. Two years later she decided to enter the Bernadette Sisters, but was refused admission because of poor health. When I arrived in Nyabihanga in September 1976, she was living with her brother on their small family farm. Her parents had died some years before. I found that even though her health had improved, the Sisters still refused to accept her. As for all Washubi girls, marriage seemed inevitable.

At the time I met her, Astheria was twenty-two years old and one of the cleverest young women in the village. Strong, straight-backed, and robust, she worked many hours in the bean field and banana plantation. She cooked well, and was very capable around the house. Her cheerful disposition, ready smile, warm greeting, and personal concern for all she met won everyone. Often during a lighthearted conversation she would tilt her head and laugh in a most endearing way. She loved to sing and dance. Attired in a bright, multicolored African dress, she would sway rhythmically during the traditional Washubi dances, her feet stamping out a lively beat.

Astheria was the leading singer in the Bukiriro outstation choir and occasionally taught in the adult catechumenate. Then the SCC ministry discovered and activated her many gifts and talents. She began as the song leader of Mtakuja SCC in November 1976. Then she became prayer leader of her community, and finally prayer leader of our whole outstation. During a parish seminar for prayer leaders in May 1977, Astheria gained valuable knowledge and experience that resulted in her being considered the most capable teacher from all twenty-one outstations.

After the seminar she visited all the SCCs in our outstation, participating in Bible services, encouraging the local leaders, and explaining the purpose of SCCs to all the Christians. When our elderly catechist, Salvatori Bahuwimbuye, retired at the end of 1977, Astheria was chosen as the new catechist of Bukiriro outstation, one of the few women catechists in Rulenge Diocese.

With energy and zeal Astheria plunged into her new work as catechist. She animated the whole Christian community by her selfless ministry and shining example. Cultivating on the church farm, teaching Sunday school, grade school, and adult classes; participating in all the meetings of the leaders of the SCCs; giving talks on prayer and spiritual formation; volunteering to work without pay during her first three months as a catechist—she was truly the inspiration of the whole outstation. When there was an unexpected talk to prepare or a visitor to welcome or a problem to solve, Astheria would simply say, "I am ready to help."

On one occasion the prayer leaders of Bukiriro outstation gave a demonstration meeting in Rulenge for SCC leaders from all the parishes in the diocese. The seminar participants marveled at Astheria's pastoral sense and clear explanations. One man from another part of the diocese exclaimed, "How can a Shubi woman answer so well!"

At this time there was a rethinking of the role of the catechist in the church in East Africa. Traditionally the catechist had been almost an artificial leader—a combination of the priest's "Boy Friday" and a "go-between" with the local people. As one critic observed:

There is some danger of a "clericalization" of catechists—clericalization in the sense that much of their training gives them the attitude that they are the knowledgeable ones, that they now have the faith to hand over to the people. They are trained apart from their people. In the training sessions most of the time is spent analyzing the Scriptures to be used in the liturgies and reflection meetings of the following month. There is very little attempt to analyze the situation in which the people find themselves. This is not seen as important. The catechists, when they lead the liturgies of the Sunday services, act in the same way as the priest does; he preaches, he hands over, he delivers, and he does not search or listen, he does not give the people opportunity to bear witness to the Spirit active in their lives. Perhaps the clearest sign of this danger of clericalization might be the fact that catechists are paid for their efforts. The people themselves look to them as more educated and superior in the faith and are willing to pay them for their services.

The rapid development of small communities created new opportunities for other lay ministries and expanded lay leadership so that the catechist no longer had a privileged, clerical-type role. Other local leaders began taking over some of the traditional work of the catechist. The outstation prayer leader conducted the Sunday service without a priest. The religious-education leader taught in grade school and Sunday school. The coordinator, together with the pastoral committee, made many important decisions. As a result, many catechists in Rulenge Diocese felt threatened; their power base was being shaken, and they were confused about their exact role and work.

Astheria welcomed the changes and responded positively to the new role of the catechist. In the diocesan pastoral plan based on SCCs, the catechist is first and foremost a shepherd who has the responsibility for the pastoral care of the Christians in his or her outstation, subparish, or parish. This is a much wider pastoral role than that of religion teacher, or leader of the Sunday service. Again, the catechist is the animator of the SCCs. In particular, the catechist advises the seven permanent leaders/helpers— prayer leader, religious-education leader, treasurer or promoter of self-reliance, marriage counselor, promoter of community spirit, promoter of sacraments and spirituality, and coordinator.

The catechist's pastoral work has been described as follows: (1) attend all the meetings of the leaders/helpers, and assist the chairpersons to answer questions and to find solutions to all the problems and difficulties of the SCCs; (2) conduct seminars, practice sessions, and other training programs for the leaders/helpers; (3) visit all the SCCs in order to get to understand the actual situation of the community members and to assist leaders/helpers to recognize the difficulties that confront them. In all this work the catechist's main goal is to make permanent the SCC plan. Perhaps in the future the catechist's entire work will be absorbed in the lay ministries of the SCCs.

Astheria had a special gift for examining the local situation and, to translate a Swahili phrase, "finding medicine to correct problems." By regularly visiting the Christians in their homes, she learned about their needs and concerns. Perhaps a Christian would refuse to attend the Bible service when it took place at the home of someone he or she didn't like. Or perhaps the school-children of a particular SCC had stopped doing the weekly practical action. Astheria would try to find a solution from the local situation of the people. For example, she knew that the Washubi women don't like to do things alone, so she organized the Christians in groups to fetch water to make bricks or to weed on the church farm—building on the African values of togetherness and community. In going to the Bible service or common work Astheria would form a little procession to pass by the homes of hesitant Christians and encourage them to "join the rest of us." As a result of these and other creative approaches, many more people participated in activities of the SCCs.

As her catechetical work flourished, Astheria faced a crisis in her personal life. Her request to enter the African Sisters was again refused. In the Bukiriro area there was mounting pressure for her to get married. Among the Washubi it was unheard of for a woman not to get married. Astheria herself admitted that she couldn't remain in Bukiriro without marrying. Psychologically and socially it would be too difficult.

At this time Bishop Christopher began developing his plan of integrated communities in Rulenge Diocese—priests, religious, laymen and laywomen, married and single, old and young living together. In such a community a young African man or woman could remain single for the Lord. The community would support the person's vocation and commitment. This was a radical new step in African society where everyone is expected to marry and raise many children. Yet the bishop had the courage and vision to propose a new option.

In September 1978 Astheria (together with four single men and three couples with children) entered the Integrated Community. She has since gone to West Germany to study for three years. Uncertain about the future, but confident in the Spirit, she is ready to travel a new path in the church in Africa.

Glimpses into an African Christian Spirituality

One Sunday three visitors came to Bukiriro outstation to participate in the Eucharist. Our local Christian community welcomed them and invited them to share in the liturgy. The guests felt at home. During the general intercessions one Christian spontaneously prayed: "We thank God for sending us our three visitors. May they have a pleasant stay here and a safe return to their homes." After the Eucharist the three visitors mingled with the Christians outside our small church, talking informally and sharing the latest news. Then some young women and schoolgirls formed a half-circle and performed traditional Washubi dances. A spirit of song and celebration filled the air. This was the local Christians' way of sharing their life and faith with the visitors.

This experience at Bukiriro taught me a great deal about the meaning of African Christian spirituality. For the African, religion and life are one. A deep religious sense permeates all life. The hospitality, the spontaneous petition, the informal sharing, and the traditional dancing were all part of the same spiritual experience. The dances were traditional dances first performed many years ago by Africans who had never heard of Christ. Performed by the Bukiriro Christian community, these dances became a sign of their Christian spirituality, a celebration of their Christian life. What made the dancing a specifically Christian spiritual experience was not the what (the dances), but the who and why (the local Christians consciously celebrating their joy and unity).

Some time later one of the visitors wrote:

> For an African, religion and daily life are one and the same reality. The marketplace can be a place of worship. Bearing one another's burdens and enjoying life together, both are expressions of faith. Working together, sharing, dancing together—everything is meant to transform this earth into a place where God is present among his people.

In the West, we have departmentalized religion, making it into a series of activities—saying prayers, attending the Eucharist on

Sunday, reading a spiritual book. Our Western logic has divided our faith into a series of distinctions and categories. John Mbiti points out that in Africa "because traditional religions permeate all the departments of life, there is no formal distinction between the sacred and the secular, between the religious and non-religious, between the spiritual and the material areas of life." In other words, spirituality is life.

Bishop Peter Sarpong describes the integration of African spirituality in this way: "To the African, religion is like the skin that you carry along with you wherever you are, not like the cloth that you wear now and discard the next moment."

That Sunday when visitors came to Bukiriro spurred me to search deeper into the various expressions of African Christian spirituality. Different ages, places, and cultures have their own spirituality, and the development of African Christian spirituality is one part of the encounter between Christianity brought by Western missionaries and African traditional religions.

The development of African Christian spirituality (like African theology) is part of the slow emergence of African Christianity. Until now Christianity has not had strong roots in the African culture. It has not yet penetrated deeply into the religious world of traditional African life. In the lives of many African Christians, Christianity is seen as an overcoat rather than an inner living reality. Thus we have only glimpses into a genuine African Christian spirituality.

An essential part of the spirituality of African traditional religions is communal relationships—relationship to God, to the ancestors, and to other people. To the African, God is Creator. God is not an abstract, metaphysical being but the source of all life and all things in the world. God is behind every event and often comes to us through nature, ancestors, and other intermediaries.

Community in traditional African cultures is not simply a community of the living. It transcends death, both through the immortality of the "living-dead" (an appropriate name for ancestors) and by the transmission of life to future generations. As Mbiti explains: "The living-dead is a person who is physically dead but alive in the memory of those who knew him in life as well as being alive in the world of the spirits. So long as the living-dead is thus remembered, he is in the state of personal immortality."

African traditional spirituality focuses on continuity with the past. The people want to be in harmony with their ancestors and carry out the rites of their ancestors in the appropriate places. This is a pledge of future divine favor. The ancestors themselves are intermediaries.

We note, then, that maintaining good relationships with one another is connected to the emphasis on the extended family and the corporate personality. An African is first and foremost a member of the community and, second, an individual. His or her life is always geared to the well-being of the community. Human life is shared, a sharing of oneself and one's goods. Being at the service of, and available to, other people is primary. Fraternity and friendship are priorities. It is very important for an African to live at peace with his or her community.

Communal relationships are a distinctive feature of the African Christian spirituality. The Christians want to be in harmony with God, their ancestors, and one another. In the traditional naming ceremony, the child is incorporated into the clan community, which comprises the living and the living-dead. Baptism symbolizes sharing in the death and resurrection of Jesus Christ and incorporation into the community of Christians. Receiving a Christian name and/or a traditional African name at baptism is a sign of power and protection, for the saints are considered to be powerful Christian ancestors. Death is a rite of passage, and a villager wants the deceased person to look kindly on him or her. Attending a funeral puts a person in a proper relationship with the deceased. It follows that the celebration of All Saints' Day and All Souls' Day is an important way of maintaining good relationships with Christian ancestors and family ancestors.

Two other experiences helped me to understand this relationship dimension of African Christian spirituality. Several times I visited the Trappist Monastery in Lumbwa, Kenya. Though the monastery was founded by Dutch Trappists, the monks now are mostly Africans from Kenya, Tanzania, and Uganda. At first the monastery closely followed the contemplative Cistercian tradition of Western Europe. Yet the African postulants and novices often broke the rule of silence while walking in the enclosure. They told the Dutch abbot, "We Africans are accustomed to greet each other. To pass by silently with heads down is against our traditional custom." After some time the abbot allowed the African monks to talk. He clearly saw that the silence rule had been imposed by Western monasticism and doesn't necessarily fit the African culture.

The experiences of the Trappists at Lumbwa further indicated that the eremitical nature of strict contemplative life is not understood in Africa. Solitude and silence clash with African community values. The Dutch abbot once told me that the Trappists need an African Saint Bernard of Clairvaux who would incarnate contemplative life in African culture. As one small step the monks at Lumbwa now have more contact with the villagers in the surrounding area. The African monks have stressed that the monastery cannot exist in isolation, but must be part of the wider community.

In the African tradition it is important that each person has a chance to speak. As a result, repetition is very common. For the Westerner, repeating the same thing many times may seem unnecessary, but in Africa it is important that each person has a say. I once celebrated the Eucharist for the intention of the Postulant Mistress of the Immaculate Heart Sisters (a Tanzanian Congregation) who was making her final vows. During the general intercessions each of the twelve postulants gave her own petition of the professed Sister. Most of these intentions were the same: asking God's blessing for the Sister; but it was important for each postulant to give her own petition as an expression of her regard and concern for the Postulant Mistress. The person, not the message or content, was the heart of the repetition.

Another significant dimension of communal relationships as a spiritual value is the development of African humanism. African humanism tries to harmonize African values with Christian values. Julius Nyerere's *Ujamaa* socialism and Kenneth Kaunda's Zambian humanism articulate a political philosophy rooted in spiritual values. African humanism gives a new application and dynamism to the human values of the ancient village world of Africa—particularly the ideas of cooperative living and sharing life together.

Nyerere started to link the rural village world of traditional African society to the villagization plan of post-independent Africa. Bishop Mwoleka has made the further link to the life of service and sharing of the SCCs. The SCCs are an African way of living gospel values within the government plan of *Ujamaa* and villagization. African Christian spirituality is expressed through the unity of life—the harmony of body and soul, material and spiritual, secular and sacred. Every moment is a spiritual experience and every action has a spiritual interpretation. Within the context of small communities Mwoleka emphasizes that "spirituality is living for others." He says, "What makes cultivating [that is, farming] a spiritual concern is that we cultivate for the benefit of our neighbor; in this way cultivating creates a relationship between us and our neighbors; it enhances love; it builds the kingdom of God."

It is crucial to see the link between the spirituality of the African traditional religions and the Christian spirituality of African Christian communities. Traditionally, community values are the most important values underlying ancestor veneration. The term "ancestor" refers to those who have died in adulthood (often meaning a full human being who has gone through the whole process of physical birth, naming ceremonies, puberty and initiation rites, and finally marriage and procreation), one who has played a major part in the service of the community. The final respect that the living-dead receive is based on their own contributions to the community.

The spirituality of the SCCs is rooted in Jesus Christ's new commandment of love and service. Members of the SCCs live out their Christian spirituality by unselfishly reaching out to others in the community, especially the poor and needy, and in this service of the community we find the link integrating gospel values with traditional African values.

The community dimension of African Christian spirituality is also expressed through spontaneity and joint participation in the African liturgy. African Christians actively participate in the Eucharist, Bible services, and other devotions, expressing their joy and enthusiasm through movement and rhythm. The Christian community prays through drumming, dancing, swaying, clapping, and ululation (a traditional way of trilling with the tongue). Unlike many Westerners, African Christians like long ceremonies with many songs (using all the stanzas) and spontaneous petitions. Praying is not a formal exercise but a living communion with God. The dramatic expansion of the African Independent churches is in part a reaction against the formalism of the institutional churches.

Another belief of African traditional spirituality is that divine power is transmitted through secondary causes, that is, God does not intervene in the lives of people directly, but through nature, the ancestors, and various signs. To the African every event is a sign of God's presence. God doesn't have to be called upon. God is already present. While Westerners are very scientific and have natural explanations for unusual events, Africans believe that God is in control of everything. Many times in Nyabihanga I heard the villagers say, "It's in God's hands," or "If God wishes." Thomas Namwaga, a Tanzanian priest from Mwanza, told me, "Many Africans are not used to pursuing the logical and ultimate reasons or causes of events taking place around them. They either take them for granted or attribute them to the highest cause [God]. A certain man was going to the hospital and while at the bus-stand he died. A hotelkeeper who witnessed the event was asked by a radio reporter how and why that man had died. He answered by saying, 'It is only by God's action that he died.' "

In the traditional African view concrete events are signs of God's involvement. For example, rain is a sign of God's favor; barrenness in a woman is a sign of God's disfavor. The African people are in such harmony with nature, which is God's creation, that God communicates to the people through nature—sun, rain, birds, animals.

A final theme of the spirituality of African traditional religions is the world of the spirits. During my two years in Nyabihanga I learned how deep and influential a part of the people's lives this is, though I understand only a small part of the spirit-oriented belief systems of the local people and the complexity of witchcraft. Gradually I discovered that even among the local Christians the influence of witchcraft is often greater than the influence of Christian values. One of our best Christian schoolboys was involved in a case with a man from another area of Tanzania. The man said his father was a powerful witch doctor and would kill the boy if he didn't confess a certain action. The schoolboy's older brother advised him to lie, saying, "It is better to lie than to die." So the boy lied during the investigation of the case. Later he told me that he knew lying was wrong and against his Christian faith, but he was really afraid.

Many experiences taught me that we can easily make moral judgments about certain African traditions without understanding the real situation. Astheria explained to me that the Washubi use the word *miungu* (literally "gods") for the people who have died in a person's clan. These ancestors are not gods in our Western sense. They are *mizimu*, or the spirits of a dead person or ancestor. And more, they are the living-dead. Since it is hard for a Westerner to understand these African traditions, we need to be open and nonjudgmental.

In this connection a basic question is how African Christian spirituality is related to the whole world of spirits. One African told me that the charismatic movement and a renewed devotion to the Holy Spirit offer a great hope for the church in Africa. He explained that the "evil spirit cult" works on the fears of the people. Witch doctors exploit the superstitions of villagers. Christians can explain that the Holy Spirit frees people from fear and brings peace of heart. This will foster a personal relationship with the "Living God." He quoted a Ugandan proverb: "Where there is love, there is no fear."

Many of these themes of African traditional religions and values of African culture have been incarnated in contemporary African Christian prayers. The language and references are vivid, concrete, and down-to-earth. In the penitential section of the Zaire Rite for the Mass the celebrant prays:

Lord our God, like the insect that sticks onto our skin and sucks our blood, evil has come upon us. Our living power has weakened. Who can save us? Is it not you, O Father? Lord have mercy.

A Tanzanian Eucharistic Prayer, based on a prayer of the Luguru people, begins:

You, Father God,
Who are in the Heavens and below,
Creator of everything and omniscient,
Conserver of the earth and the sky;

We are but little children;
Unknowing anything evil,
We entreat your mercy.
Also you, our Grandparents,
Who sleep in the place of light,
All ancestors, men and women, great and small,
Help us, have compassion on us,
So that we can also sleep peacefully.

The christological part of the Eucharistic Prayer of the Zaire Rite reads:

Holy Father, we praise you through your Son Jesus Christ, our mediator. He is your Word, the Word that gives life. Through him, you created our river, the Zaire. Through him you created our forests, our rivers, our lakes. Through him you created the animals who live in our forests, and the fish who live in our rivers. Through him you created the things we see, and also the things we do not see.

In an All-Africa Eucharistic Prayer, the prayer over the gifts is:

Father, send the Spirit of Life,
The Spirit of power and fruitfulness.
With His breath, speak your Word into these things,
Make them the living body
And the life blood
Of Jesus, our brother!
Give us who eat and drink in your presence
Life and power and fruitfulness of heart and body;
Give us true brotherhood with your Son.

After the consecration, a Kenya Eucharistic Prayer adapts a traditional Meru prayer as follows:

Owner of all things,
We offer you this Cup in memory of your Son.
We beg you for life,
For healthy people with no disease.

May they bear healthy children.
And also for women who suffer because they are barren,
Open the way by which they may see children.
Give the good life to our parents and kinsmen
Who are with you.

In an All-Africa Eucharistic Prayer one of the concelebrants
prays:

Give us kinship and brotherhood . . .
With the living,
and the living-dead,
With children yet unborn,
In Jesus, who was anointed with the Medicine of Life.

This Eucharistic Prayer concludes with all saying:

And you, our prayer,
Prayer of the long-distant past,
You ancient Word, spoken by the Father,
You whose breath is the Spirit,
Prayer of the Ancestors,
You are spoken now! Amen!

All this research into the meaning of African Christian spirituality encouraged me to reflect more deeply on missionary spirituality, for a deep and authentic spirituality is essential for missionaries. This missionary spirituality is the total response of the
person—the process of integrating our inner convictions and the
outward expression of these convictions in our missionary life.

Most descriptions of missionary spirituality in recounting
the spiritual values of the men and women who go forth to preach
the gospel of Jesus Christ stress the qualities and attitudes the
person takes to Africa, Asia, Latin America, and other places. Yet
this neglects an essential dimension of missionary spirituality. The
heart of the missionary vocation is to love the people and their
culture. Missionaries should relinquish their home culture and
incarnate themselves into their new culture. They must "pass
over" into the experience of another—another person, another

culture, another mentality. The goal of this "pass over" is communion—the heart of incarnation.

Here we ought to appreciate the subtle but very real distinction between "spirituality for mission" and "missionary spirituality." The former has a nuance of superiority, as though we equip ourselves spiritually to go out to preach the gospel on the mission stations. The latter implies that we develop our spirituality in the context of our mission situation.

A genuine missionary spirituality means entering into the spirituality of the people and culture where one lives and works. For missionaries in Africa this means feeling at home with the various dimensions of African Christian spirituality, at ease with spontaneity, repetition, length, and related characteristics of popular religiosity. It means feeling comfortable praying with SCCs, living for others in the service of the community, and being attuned to the spiritual witness of presence rather than mere missionary activism.

Missionaries going to Africa (or any other part of the mission world) are learners more than teachers, listeners more than speakers. They are challenged to let themselves be evangelized and transformed by the local Christian spirituality and local cultural values. They are further challenged to develop a missionary spirituality that integrates missionary qualities such as restlessness, rootlessness, presence, flexibility, and a spirituality of the road with universal Christian values such as community living, a prayerful life, a simple lifestyle, apostolic work, solidarity with the poor, and action for justice.

An American missionary Brother, talking about the formative aspects of his vocation, emphasized that far more than in his novitiate training in the United States, or in his long preparation before going overseas, or in his regular spiritual exercises, he was formed in the overseas mission situation itself. He said, "Overseas I was evangelized by the poor."

Singing is an important part of the weekly Bible services and other gatherings of the SCCs. Music, storytelling, proverbs, and drama are some of the African traditional means of communication and very important for incarnating Christianity into African culture.

V

African Customs and Traditions

The girls in Bukiriro perform a traditional Washubi ethnic group dance. These dances were first used many years ago by Africans who had never heard of Christ. Performed by the Bukiriro Christian community these dances become a sign of their Christian spirituality, a celebration of their Christian

Neighbors in Nyabihanga and Bukiriro regularly visit each other to talk and share together. Home visiting illustrates the deep African values of community, personal relationships, and hospitality. These are important African Christian values as well.

Sharing a traditional Tanzanian meal of beans and bananas is an important sign of friendship and community. An African proverb says that "relationship is in the eating together." The African custom is that the visitor is always welcome.

Jet Ride on a Banana

Two months after arriving in Africa I began studying Swahili, the main language of East Africa. After a few weeks I celebrated the Eucharist in Swahili at the convent of the Immaculate Heart Sisters. In introducing myself I said, "I have come from America by 'banana' (*ndizi*)" when I meant to say "airplane" (*ndege*). The Sisters roared with laughter as they visualized a person riding on a banana. My language teacher warned me that this would not be my last mistake in Swahili. It wasn't.

Since then I have referred to the priest's "pastoral work" (*kazi ya uchungaji*) as "work of livestock and animal husbandry" (*kazi ya ufugaji*). I have mixed up "fisherman" (*mvuvi*) and "a lazy person" (*mvivu*), with embarrassing results. During a meeting at the Rulenge Seminar Center, I left the delegates saying, "I'll be back in a few days" (*siku chache*) rather than a "few minutes" (*dakika chache*).

One day as Thomas and I were cleaning our house in Nyabi-hanga, my ankles and legs suddenly began itching. We had been attacked by small insects which were all over the floor and soon all over my shoes and pants. Thomas said, "Viroboto," a Swahili word I didn't know. I was torn between slapping, scratching, and stamping to get rid of these mysterious insects and looking up the word in my Swahili-English Dictionary. Painfully, I found the answer: *viroboto* means "fleas." Though we used DDT, the fleas were the real victors. Ever since that day I have found the word hard to pronounce and often say *viboroto* instead of *viroboto*.

In Nyabihanga I encountered Shubi, the language of the Washubi people. My mistakes caused great merriment. One day a woman in the village came to sell a large tin (the equivalent of four gallons) of corn. After exchanging greetings I asked her the name of her husband, since this would easily identify the woman and her section of the village. She answered, "Bigori." When Joseph

Mukasa came to help me to settle the price, I said, "This woman is the wife of Bigori"—confidently thinking that Bigori was her husband. Joseph laughed and told me that in Shubi *bigori* means "corn." The woman thought that my Swahili question was "What are you selling?"

Soon after I arrived in Africa an Irish missionary priest who had worked for more than thirty years in Zambia told me, "Here in Africa you should live with a sense of humor and a sense of wonder." This good advice has helped me a great deal in learning and using Swahili. I am average in speaking Swahili, so I need to "grin and bear it" often. My many mistakes reveal the patience and understanding of my African listeners more than anything else.

Since the Little Brothers do not speak English, we used Swahili all the time in Nyabihanga. Surprisingly, most of the time I did not feel the need to speak English. I could go along for several weeks just using Swahili, though I confess I got tired of speaking Swahili and listening to Swahili especially in the evening. When I was physically tired I had poor concentration and made many mistakes in pronunciation. At such times many "bananas" rather than "airplanes" slipped out.

As is the way with all foreigners in East Africa, I discovered that language is much more than pronouncing Swahili words correctly and having a good memory. Swahili has its own unique characteristics linked to the local people and culture. To understand and appreciate these characteristics is to avoid a lot of worry, frustration, and misunderstanding. One needs to appreciate the difference between the exact meaning and the conventional or applied meaning of many Swahili words. For example, the Swahili word *asante* ("thank you") can have many meanings according to the circumstances or context in which it is used. *Asante* can be used in its exact meaning or context simply as "thank you"—an expression of one's gratitude to someone else who has done a favor. However, when one person insults another, the one being insulted may say, "Asante." Here the word *asante* is being used ironically and not in its exact meaning. This is also the case in Luganda and other African languages.

Ndiyo ("yes") is a Swahili word that can be used in many contexts. *Ndiyo* is sometimes called the "polite yes." The person giving consent does not really mean agreement or affirmation. Since the person is afraid of offending the other, "yes" is used nicely out of politeness.

A certain priest wanted to convert a local chief who had many wives. The priest talked about God and how he loved the world so much that he sent his only son to save the world. The priest then asked the chief if he understood and believed all this, and the chief said, "Ndiyo." When the priest asked the chief to send away his wives, the chief said that he would think it over. After some years another priest went to this chief with the same message asking the chief if he was ready for baptism. The chief said, "Ndiyo." Yet the chief died unbaptized. Since the chief respected the priests, he did not want to disappoint them by saying no to them, but he kept postponing the day of his baptism—although he had said "Ndiyo."

When I first came to Africa and asked a sick person how he (or she) felt I would get the answer, "nzuri kidogo" ("Good, a little"). I soon learned that Africans used *nzuri* as a standard reply, even though later they would qualify the meaning of "good" with other expressions. A person could be very sick and still say, "I am feeling *nzuri kidogo.*" This is part of the cheerful optimism of the African character.

The words *karibu* ("near") and *mbali* ("far") often have to be understood in a figurative or relative sense. When asking directions to a certain village I was told that it was "karibu sana" ("very near"). I drove on for five miles before actually reaching the village.

Another challenge for the missionary is to try to appreciate the cultural linguistics and feeling levels of the language. A missionary priest who speaks Swahili fluently, has excellent pronunciation and a large speaking and reading vocabulary, admits that he still has trouble "communicating" with the people. He knows the Swahili words—the form of the language—but he doesn't understand the "silent" language, the nonverbal communication, the cultural thought patterns, and the feelings of his listeners and audience. The secret of true interchange is to enter this feeling level where the deepest communication and sharing take place.

Jambo Is Only the Beginning

Many Swahili conversations begin with "Jambo," which means "How are you?" or "How do you do?" or simply "Hello." It is the commonest form of greeting in Swahili. But *jambo* is only the beginning!

In Africa the tradition of greeting is an important part of social life. Through greeting, a person starts exchanging ideas with his or her neighbor. Greeting for an African is the beginning and extension of relationship with other people. It does not require or demand any special ceremony before taking place. Its purpose is to establish a relationship, not just to get information.

When meeting someone for the first time in the day or at any particular part of the day, one should greet before saying anything else. Even when reproaches are to be made, greetings should be exchanged first. Africa has a person-centered rather than a task-oriented culture. Extended greetings are a very important part of the "small talk" before starting business.

Greeting patterns vary widely according to the ethnic group and the particular situation. The Baganda people in Uganda have a long greeting pattern. The initial exchange of greetings and informal questions and answers can be extensive, depending upon the relationship of the people involved. In Africa one of the deepest greetings is with both hands held out in friendship.

In some Western countries if two people meet for the first time, they will not greet each other until they have been introduced by a third party. Unless they have been formally introduced to each other, they could rub shoulders year in and year out in the same place without a "Good morning."

For an African such a thing would be unthinkable. When an African meets another person the first thing he does is to stop and say a few words of greeting to the person. He will ask the person how he or she is, how everyone at home spent the night, and how everyone got up in the morning. By doing so the African is creating "relationship"—extending one's circle of friends, especially if the person being greeted is from a distant region. To a foreigner all these exchanges may seem superfluous and time-consuming.

While East Africans use the word *jambo* for "How are you?" they do not use it as abruptly as some foreigners do. Many Westerners will simply say "Jambo" to an African and then disappear or be silent. Foreigners often do not stop to inquire the name of the person they are greeting, how the person feels, and so forth. To many Africans such behavior indicates that foreigners are proud, or simply do not value Africans as fellow human beings, or perhaps that they don't know the particular African language well.

John Kabeya, a Tanzanian priest from Tabora archdiocese, told me that when a person enters a circle of people and immediately starts saying "Jambo" quickly to each one, the person is probably a politician or a foreigner. It is easy to shorten greetings or eliminate them completely when we are in a hurry. Thomas Namwaga shared with me one of his personal experiences: "Once I was driving from Mwanza to a nearby town. We passed a person we knew, but we only waved without stopping to greet the person or offer him a lift. A few minutes later we had a flat tire. The other person came along on foot and offered to help us. Later he commented that we didn't have time to stop and greet him, but now we were depending on his help."

All these examples show the importance of the spoken word in Africa. It is the most basic, most common, and most important means of communication. Much of the history, many traditions and customs of African cultures are intimately connected to oral tradition. This has significant implications for evangelization and catechetics in Africa. Person-to-person conversation is the most direct way of preaching and sharing the Good News. The gospel message can be communicated in many informal, verbal ways, for example, while talking with people socially, visiting homes, and joining in the circle of village elders. Many important values are transmitted and decisions reached under the "palaver [i.e., discussion] tree." What is popularly called "Mango Tree Theology" has great relevance for African Christianity.

One of the Tanzanian bishops explained to me the importance of the oral tradition through a very practical example. He mentioned that in Western countries bishops often use a pastoral letter to communicate with the Christian people. Usually the letter is read in church on Sunday and then distributed throughout the diocese in printed form. In Africa most Christians cannot read. A printed document such as a pastoral letter is formal and impersonal. So this bishop told me that he prefers to talk with the people informally—outside the church on Sundays, in their homes, or at celebrations and meetings. This is the bishop's "pastoral walk" among his people. He communicates and shares with the Christians in the many experiences of everyday life—joining with the Christian community in family life, work life, recreation, and various social occasions. He stresses interpersonal relationships and social values rather than information and formal religious instruction.

Experience with communications patterns in Tanzania shows that the Western method of direct questions and answers is foreign to many people in Africa. Africans have a much more casual and indirect style of using questions, for example, as part of lengthy greetings: "How did you spend the night?" "How is your home?" "How are your children?" It is not customary to ask questions purely for information. People might give the answer that they think you want rather than the correct answer.

I once accompanied Bishop Mwoleka on a census of the Christians in Nyabihanga village. Even though he knew many of the people and used Shubi, the local language, the bishop had trouble getting exact information from the people, for example, the number of children in a family (children who have died often are included in the total number given), which children belong to which wives, details about baptism, and so on.

Another time in Nyabihanga, Little Brother Fabian tried to sort out a marriage case. After one-half hour of asking questions he gave up, saying that he knew less about the case at the end of the question period than at the beginning. Even Astheria, who knew the Washubi customs and traditions very well, had trouble getting specific information about religious matters from the Christians.

A Western research style can be misleading, even disastrous in Africa. Many Africans are not comfortable with the cold, impersonal style of a questionnaire. A person-to-person interview is often more effective, but even here "Jambo" is only the beginning.

The Many Meanings of *Zamani*

During a two-month period in Nyabihanga village, I wrote down the different uses of the Swahili word *zamani* ("long ago" or "a period of time"). *Zamani* was used to refer to:

2000 years ago—the birth of Christ
10 years ago—the writing of the Arusha Declaration
last year—the time a certain man moved into the village
3 weeks ago—when the head of Rulenge District visited Nyabihanga
last week—when we finished planting corn
yesterday—when a schoolboy recovered from malaria
15 minutes ago—when Athanasius finished a cup of tea

I noticed that the villagers pronounced *zamani* with different stresses according to different time periods. They lengthened or prolonged the accented middle syllable to indicate a longer time ago, as *za-maaaa-ni.*

This experience with the spoken language helped me to understand the meaning of time in African society. While different ethnic groups and different languages in Africa have their unique characteristics, there are many common patterns connected with the culture and the oral traditions. The traditional African concept of time is two-dimensional, with a long past, a present, and virtually no future. The linear concept of time in the West, with an indefinite past, a present, and an infinite future, is practically foreign to Africans. Unlike the period which in English we call "the past," *zamani* means the unlimited past having its own "past," "present," and "future" on a wider scale. *Sasa* ("now") covers the now period or now moment and has the sense of the immediate and near. The future is very brief. The traditional African concept of time does not conceive of the distant future; since it has not been experienced, it does not really constitute an element in time.

The past and present dominate the African understanding of the individual, community, and universe. Actual time moves backward rather than forward. History moves from the *sasa* period to the *zamani* period. Since the future does not exist beyond a few months, "the end of the world" and "a new world to come" have no meaning. Rather, everything disappears into *zamani,* in which a person after death is remembered as one of the living-dead.

Other time words in Swahili indicate that African time is flexible and relative. An expression that can sometimes cause misunderstanding is *sasa hivi* ("just now" or "right now"). Thomas Namwaga gave me this example: "A few days ago I was looking for a priest who had come to visit us in Mwanza. When I asked a priest at Mwanza Cathedral, where the visitor was, I was told, "He has left just now." One-half hour later during lunch I asked another priest who had been with the visitor. He told me, 'That priest has left just now.' I was a little vexed by the answer, because I knew that the visiting priest had left one-half hour before, and yet that lapse of time was still *sasa hivi*."

If you are hurrying to the Serengeti Game Park and the spring of your car breaks, you might be consoled by the garage mechanic who says that your car will be repaired *sasa hivi.* Your expectation to leave very soon, however, can turn into a big disappointment when after an hour or so the spring is not yet fixed or replaced with a new one. In such a case the words *sasa hivi* are used by convention and for the sake of encouragement.

Another time word is *baadaye* ("afterward"). Depending on the situation and context it can mean "after a short time" or "after a long time." *Kesho* ("tomorrow") has similar flexibility and variability. Very often it does not mean the twenty-four hour period starting at midnight tonight. It means some time in the future—tomorrow, in three days, next week, and so forth. Out of politeness a person might say, "I will come *kesho*" ("tomorrow") referring to some time in the near future.

One Kenyan priest told me, "Time does not exist in the Reserve [the traditional African area]." Many Africans in rural areas tell the time by the sun rather than by a watch or clock. Time is based on two twelve-hour periods each day. The daylight period follows the sun. What is "8 A.M." in the West is "two hours" in East Africa (or two hours after the sun has risen as indicated by raising one's arm to follow the rising sun on the horizon). Knowing the exact time and following a precise schedule are not important. A person can save a lot of worry and frustration by adjusting to this fluid time pattern. What does "Mass will start at 10 A.M." mean to people who do not have a watch, especially those in rural areas? Local government leaders may call a meeting for 8:00 A.M. but the people arrive at 9:00 A.M. or 10:00 A.M. or even 11:00 A.M. Everyone seems to adjust to this flexible timetable.

In Africa, time does not have the focused meaning that obtains where everything has to be planned down to the last second. The African people have a slower, more relaxed pace. Time is not money, so there is more time for interpersonal relationships and social activities.

In explaining how the African concept of time is the key to understanding basic religious and philosophical concepts, John Mbiti offers this insight:

> In Western or technological society, time is a commodity which must be utilized, sold, and bought; but in traditional African life time has to be created or produced. Man is not a slave of time; instead he "makes" as much time as he wants. When foreigners, especially from Europe and America, come to Africa and see people sitting down somewhere without, evidently, doing anything, they often remark, "These Africans waste their time by just sitting down idle!" Another common cry is, "Oh, Africans are always late!" It is easy to jump to such judgments, but they are judgments based on ignorance of what time means to African people. Those who are seen sitting down, are actually not wasting time, but either waiting for time or in the process of "producing" time.

Missionaries and other foreigners working in Africa are challenged to enter into this time framework of the African way of life. Part of this is learning to appreciate the "timelessness" of social occasions and personal relationships. Once I attended a big celebration to welcome the new Mother General of the Immaculate Heart Sisters. The songs, dances, plays, and poetry readings lasted for five hours. The Tanzanians seemed very happy to participate in the whole celebration. At the beginning I counted over twenty missionary priests, Brothers, Sisters, and lay people. As the hours went on, the foreigners began to leave one or two at a time. At the end only three of us were left. I turned to an American Sister and admitted that I had remained out of sheer determination. She mentioned that she had thoroughly enjoyed the whole celebration and wasn't conscious of the time passing. She was caught up in the present moment. She had discovered African timelessness.

In August 1978 we prepared to travel to the north part of Rulenge Diocese for the first Sunday Eucharist of one of the newly ordained Tanzanian priests. The other Tanzanian priests wanted to leave on Thursday to participate in the preparations and celebrations before the liturgy itself. Several of the missionaries could not understand why the Africans were going so early. One of them said, "If we arrive on Saturday afternoon we will be in plenty of time." He saw the Eucharist as a specific religious event, while the Tanzanians saw the whole weekend as a social experience.

The African feeling toward time results in a relaxed attitude toward life that is not controlled by urgency and pressure. One missionary priest in Tanzania wrote:

I am making five-year plans in a rural community whose remote future doesn't go beyond the next harvest, or the next rainy season, that is, six months at the most. [I say that] time is pressing, we must act quickly, tomorrow will be too late. And so I push and push, I get impatient, and I come up against a polite wall of silence, a rubber wall, pliable, flexible, but impenetrable. If I push too strongly, the wall will bounce me backward, and I am liable to do myself an injury as I fall. Once again I wanted to impose my views, my feelings or urgency, until the day a friend gently told me, "Why do you weep before your grandmother is dead?" As for me, I am thinking, "Perhaps there is still time to save grandmother if we act quickly." But it is not my grandmother, it is his.

For the African, time is closely connected to person-centered values. This is quite different from the Western view where time is usually functional. In the West we are caught up in the "don't waste time" and "immediately if not sooner" syndromes. An Irish missionary priest who was turning over his office to an African priest was aware of their different styles of work. He noticed that the African sometimes didn't do all the desk work and filing, but he spent a lot more time with visitors. The missionary observed, "The African priest doesn't do forty percent of the work that I do, but I don't do eighty percent of the work that he does." A lot of the African successor's invisible work was connected with relationships. His goal was people.

In general Africans do not anticipate future events and activities. They live one day at a time. I discovered this while living with the schoolboys, Thomas, John, and Christopher. They never worried about a reserve supply. If they received a gift of four pounds of fresh meat, they would eat it immediately without thinking how the precious meat could be spaced over three or four days. When they ran out of firewood, they would simply go out and collect more wood for that day. They rarely anticipated a rainy day or unexpected visitors. They lived intuitively rather than systematically.

Africa, however, is in transition and the traditional African concept of time is changing. Schools, factories, office jobs, and especially the conditions of urban life are making people much more time conscious. Long meetings and long ceremonies are becoming less frequent. A Kenyan priest told me that once he was officiating at a burial service in Nairobi. Under the burning sun the speeches for the deceased went on and on. The priest was hot, tired, and thirsty. When finally the priest was called upon to say a prayer, all he could think of was to pray for rain.

I'll Walk You Home

About 6 A.M. on a crisp April morning we said goodbye to Little Brother Emmanuel. He was returning to his home in Burundi for a vacation. He had decided to enter Burundi on foot at the border town of Muhinga, twenty miles from Nyabihanga. As we exchanged farewells at the Little Brothers' house, Thomas said he would *sindikiza* ("accompany" or "escort") Emmanuel for part of his journey. After breakfast the rest of us worked in the fields until lunch. Thomas did not return until about 1 P.M. He had accompanied Emmanuel as far as Rwinyana, a village seven miles from Nyabihanga. All together Thomas had walked fourteen miles to say goodbye. This was a witness to the core value of maintaining relationships. The amount of time spent, the personal discomfort, the work that was left behind were all secondary considerations. The person came first.

This *sindikiza* custom is perhaps the most fascinating of all African customs. It is an example of many African values and priorities—personal relationships, sharing, community, hospitality, and gratitude. When I first arrived in Africa I was told that this accompanying or escorting custom was very, very old. In rural areas when friends came to visit, the host would walk them half-way back to their home or next destination as a gesture of respect. Part of the tradition says that if lions or other wild animals are prowling about, accompanying visitors protects them until they get near their own village and familiar ground.

I have many memories of *sindikiza* experiences in Africa: friends escorting me to the Tanzanian border the day I left Rulenge; a crowd of villagers running alongside Bishop Mwoleka's Land-Rover as he left Nyabihanga, the children sprinting in a cloud of dust until the car was out of sight; the Bukiriro Christians accompanying the new catechist to the bus stop as he started his journey to the catechists' school; my neighbors passing the bishop's house with friends who were returning to the next village; the schoolboys escorting members of a nearby SCC after they had attended the Nyabuliga weekly Bible service.

During a vacation in America in 1972 I visited the Tanzanian ambassador to the United States, whose daughter is a Theresian Sister in Bukoba. It was a cold February afternoon, but when I prepared to leave, the ambassador's wife (he had left for a meeting) insisted on accompanying me to my car. I protested, but she said quietly, "It is our custom." Then she laughed and told me how her American friends say goodbye to her on cold or rainy days. They peer through the small glass panel in the front door and wave goodbye without stepping out into the cold or rain.

An American priest working in a black parish in Detroit told me about one of his home visitations. After talking with a black woman in her apartment the priest prepared to leave. The woman insisted on walking the priest not only down to the front door of the apartment house, but the two blocks back to his rectory. She was living out a custom of her African roots.

A Zairean priest, Benedict Kabongo, explained this relationship priority as the key to many attitudes and actions of Africans:

> The African lives and wants personal relationships. Because the European is job-oriented, he is a methodical prisoner of his plan and his time. The African, on the other hand, in his search for relationships, often fails to take a decision for fear of displeasing someone—he fails to make precise plans in order to be able to accommodate everyone. The European, in single-mindedly following his plan, cannot readily understand his worker or driver who makes a detour to go say hello to a friend or to visit a relative. While the European counts the time lost and the expense involved in the detour, the Zairois is happy to have used that time in what for him is of essence—maintaining ties. For him money is meant to create relationships—ties that are a source of security. That's why he finds thrift so difficult.

An everyday custom in one country or culture can be unknown in another country or culture, as I discovered in a humorous way when I went to lunch with Jael Mbogo in Nairobi. I had been trained to hold the chair of a woman before sitting down at a table. So when Jael and I walked up to a luncheon table with four places, I spontaneously stepped behind the chair nearest to Jael. Thinking that I wanted to sit in that chair Jael moved to the next chair. I followed her—intent on holding her chair. Still thinking that I wanted that chair she moved to the third chair and finally back to the first chair. I followed each time. Finally we both laughed, realizing that we had made a full circle around the table.

Two African Marriages

Andrea Ngenzi's wedding was a big event in Bukiriro outstation. Andrea, the brother of our catechist Astheria, was one of the most promising young men in our area. He had already "made good," having learned carpentry in Mwanza and started a permanent, salaried job in Rulenge.

Since there were only three or four church weddings a year each one was a major social and religious occasion. I celebrated the wedding Mass on a warm, Saturday morning in October. Our small outstation church was packed. The enthusiastic choir had practiced new songs for the special day. Andrea wore a new, long-sleeved blue shirt, open at the collar. His bride, Scholastica, wore *Kitenge*, a traditional African cloth, which is a bright, multicolored cotton fabric, one piece of which she wore as a dress, and one piece as a veil. She looked shy, but deeply happy.

Andrea and Scholastica's wedding had been planned months in advance. Just five days before the wedding the parish priest, Father Lazaro, told me that another young couple, Andrea and Helena, from a neighboring outstation, would be getting married at Bukiriro on the same day. My immediate reaction was that Andrea and Scholastica would be disappointed at having to share the limelight with another couple. I was wrong. Andrea was pleased that the two weddings could take place together. He told me that this showed the African value of community.

At the wedding Helena wore a white gown. No doubt Helena and many Africans thought these were the right clothes to wear; the proper church wedding required a white wedding gown and flower girls. Yet in this hot, dusty African outstation Western-style dress seemed incongruous.

After reading the Gospel I stood in front of the two couples to begin the official marriage ceremony itself. I looked at these two Tanzanian brides—Scholastica in her African *Kitenge* cloth, Helena in her Western white gown. In a single moment this scene dramatized for me the basic dilemma in African Christianity today. The two brides were like actresses on a contemporary stage. Scholastica in her blue, orange, and brown African dress symbolized the search to Africanize Christianity. Helena in her store-bought white gown symbolized the strong tradition to Christianize Africa.

This same drama is being acted out in many places in Africa. Some of the actors are important leaders who have encouraged the development of African Christianity. Standing on African soil in 1969 Pope Paul VI stressed: "You Africans are from now on your own missionaries. That is to say, you Africans must continue to build the church in this continent. . . . You may and you must have an African Christianity." Again, speaking to the African bishops in 1977, the pope said, "Christianity can and must be entirely 'at home' in African cultures." These same bishops forcefully stated:

> The Bishops of Africa and Madagascar consider as being completely out-of-date, the so-called theology of adaptation. In its stead, they adopt the theology of incarnation. The young churches of Africa and Madagascar cannot refuse to face up to this basic demand. They accept the fact of theological pluralism within the unity of faith, and consequently they must encourage, by all means, African theological research. Theology must be open to the aspiration of the people of Africa if it is to help Christianity to become incarnate in the life of the peoples of the African continent. To achieve this, the young churches of Africa and Madagascar must take over more and more responsibility for their own evangelization and total development.

The AMECEA Study Conference in August 1979 stressed that SCCs are the best means for developing African Christianity:

> Small communities also seem to be the most effective means of making the Gospel message truly relevant to African cultures and traditions. By participating in the life of the church at this most local level, Christians will foster the gradual and steady maturing of the young church. As their sense of responsibility for the church grows, ordained and nonordained Christians will discover the meaning of a truly African expression of the Christian faith.

Cardinal Joseph Malula of Zaire states that "yesterday the foreign missionaries Christianized Africa; today the Christians of Africa are invited to Africanize Christianity." Cardinal Paul Zoungrana of Upper Volta, one of the most articulate spokesmen of the Catholic church in Africa, emphasizes the African church's originality and its "very legitimate desire to work for a Christianity that assumes African values and finds authentic African forms of expression."

There are clear signs of the gradual development of an African Christianity. Liturgical experimentation includes the Zairean Eucharistic Rite, creative use of drums, dance, and symbolic vestments in Cameroon, and African Eucharistic Prayers in Eastern Africa. The rapid growth of "small Christian communities with a human face" offer many opportunities for a grassroots church to grow out of the African soil.

On this same African stage are actors who discourage the development of genuine African Christianity. Many African Christians, including bishops and priests, resist the incarnation of the Christian life and message in African culture. A significant African theology is only now developing. The institutional church is slow and cautious in supporting experimentation in many places in Africa.

Part of this problem can be traced to historical factors. When the missionaries first began to preach the gospel in Africa, they presented a European form of Christianity as the ideal. Western Christianity was an expression of the superior Western civilization. Many Africans turned from their "pagan" ways and "primitive" culture to embrace Christianity as the true religion. Until today many expressions of Western Christianity still dominate the Africa church: pictures of sweet Italian Madonnas, stained-glass windows, large churches of foreign design, centralized parish organization, a canon-law mentality. The Second Vatican Council and different synods of bishops have called for a genuine universalism, but the African church has responded cautiously. In certain dioceses the missionaries have introduced experimentation and the incarnation of Christianity into African culture faster than local priests, religious, and lay people have. Many Africans seem embarrassed and unwilling to embrace their own culture and traditions in music (songs and instruments), symbols, and various local customs. There is still a strong feeling that these African cultural elements are bad, or at least inferior to the Western ideal.

The dilemma in evolving an authentic African Christianity is graphically symbolized in the controversy over the "Black Christ." While working as the Social Communications Secretary of AMECEA, I often presented slides and pictures of Christ portrayed as an African. Two moving examples were "Preaching the Good News in Malawi Today," a sound/slide series in which a Malawian carpenter plays the part of Jesus, and "Life of Jesus Mafa," colored pictures based on scenes of the life of Jesus as dramatized by African Christians in Cameroon. But there were always strong feelings for and against Christ appearing as an African.

For some, the search of the African church for maturity and relevance is to see Christ and his church as African. Africans can best believe and understand the Christ of faith through their own culture and traditions. This means portraying Jesus in African signs and symbols.

P. Pondy explains this eloquently:

It is urgent and necessary for us to proclaim and to express the message, the life, and the whole person of Jesus Christ in an African artistic language, in our language which is the expression of our daily life, of our culture. Many people of different cultures have done it before us and will do it in the future, without betraying the historical Christ, from whom all authentic Christianity arises. We must not restrict ourselves to the historical and cultural forms of a particular people or period.

The creation of a Black Christ in Africa does not diminish at all the historical Christ; on the contrary, it enriches the universal meaning of the message of God who became one of us in order to proclaim Christ as Lord of all nations of the world through all their authentic riches: their languages, their gestures, their art, their whole life and culture which are God's gifts and should be returned to Him as a cultural offering.

Others want to present the historical Jesus as accurately as possible—a white non-African in a non-African setting. They say that the Black Christ is false, misleading, and a harmful adaptation. This view often reflects the African people's uneasiness and "complex" about the positive values in African customs and traditions.

During communications workshops and seminars in Eastern

Africa we often stressed the importance of the African traditional means of communications—drama, dance, music, drums, and storytelling. During one workshop a Kenyan artist movingly described his feelings while painting Jesus as an African. He said that he experienced Jesus in a deeper and more meaningful way through African culture and symbols, and he wanted to share his experience of the African Christ through art. A Ugandan playwright described his similar vision of dramatizing the life of Jesus in plays that have African settings.

The AMECEA Pastoral Institute in Kenya has achieved a great deal toward incarnating Christianity in African culture, especially through liturgy, religious education, and community lifestyle. In writing about "group media" one of the specialists of the institute said:

> The African traditional means of communication are the most effective group media in the service of inculturation. . . . Within the realm, then, of the traditional media and the performing arts, we find a tremendous wealth of material to be used as media in a group process. Poetry, rhythm, dance, music, storytelling, proverbs and riddles, drama, all performed by the group for the group, are most valuable elements in our work of inculturation. In using these media for self-expression, our people are able to develop authentic and creative art forms, which are bound to bear fruit in our liturgies and forms of worship, rooting our Christian faith ever more firmly in Africa's soil.

Specific uses of these African traditional means of communication include the following: liturgical celebrations, in which dance can express joy, sorrow, suffering, service, community, and other gospel values; animal stories (rabbit stories, for examples are very popular in rural Africa), linked to religious truths, both entertain and educate; gospel plays, pageants, and pantomimes create great audience interest and participation. In these and other examples the group members assist one another in developing a deeper understanding of the Christian message in the African life situation; often the group translates this understanding into practical action.

The incarnation of Christianity into African culture takes on new meaning through a deeper understanding of the image of the "seeds of the Word" present in African culture. Cardinal Maurice Otunga of Kenya explains:

> Religion and culture, in Africa as elsewhere, are never separated from one another. Therefore, the culture, or rather, cultures of the African people possess "seeds of the Word" that could well give a tremendous contribution to the universal church. Before the Second Vatican Council, African cultural and religious heritage was seen as a *preparatio evangelii*. What this meant was that as soon as evangelization started, the whole wealth of cultural tradition was set aside. However, the Council Fathers created a new and more dynamic image, that of the *semina verbi*. In this new image, Christ is seen as the new sower who has already planted seeds in African cultural tradition. . . .
>
> The basis for the incarnation of the Christian message into our African cultures is our faith in the Incarnate Son of God. This is the most compelling reason why the gospel message must be integrated with African culture. A truly local church will emerge from the use of a life-centered catechesis that will make it possible for the gospel to be rooted in the lives of our African people.

The image of the "seeds of the Word" is biblical and makes a deep impression on the African people, who live so close to the land. Christ is the sower who has already planted in African culture seeds that can produce flowers never seen before. When the African people open themselves to the Good News of Jesus Christ, while at the same time preserving their cultural identity, the whole church is enriched with new values and insights. Some of my most exciting moments in Africa have been spent in participating in the development of African Christianity—watching African flowers grow in African soil. In Nyabihanga, African proverbs, sayings, and stories are often genuine seeds of the Word. The songs and celebrations of planting time, harvest time, and other festivals, incorporated into the Christian liturgy, recognized the natural rhythms of African life. Our biggest congregations in Bukiriro were always gatherings to participate in the eucharistic celebrations to bless the seeds before planting, or to offer thanksgiving for the first fruits during the harvest season. At such times the Eucharist took place outdoors. All were invited to bring their seeds—villagers who belonged to African traditional religions as well as Christians. They placed their baskets and containers of seeds—beans, corn, millet, peanuts, cassava—around the altar. We sang special songs and used special prayers. After the blessing of the seeds, we proceeded to a nearby field. As a symbolic gesture I sprinkled holy water to the four corners of the village. This spoke deeply to the Tanzanian farmers. They are not hyphenated persons. Their religion and their farming are one life. Their Christianity and their culture are integrated.

Although a genuine African Christianity is emerging rather slowly in Tanzania, I saw many hopeful signs of a real incarnational approach, especially in Africanizing the liturgy and catechesis. Formerly customs of Western Christianity were imposed on Africa to the point of obliterating the richness of the religious traditions of African society. Now genuine African customs are gradually replacing Western customs. One example concerns sitting during the reading of the Gospel. In the African tradition, when a powerful chief sent his messengers to each village, the villagers would sit in an open area near the center of the village. The messenger would stand in their midst and announce the chief's news. So too with the Gospel. The reader stands in the midst of the Christian community, which is seated. He proclaims the Good News of Jesus Christ as announced by one of God's four messengers, the evangelists.

Many Western customs connected with Holy Week services are strange to African Christians. I have seen countless methods of reverencing the cross on Good Friday. A neighboring outstation relates this to the culture of the local people. Each person quietly approaches the crucifix, bows, and then gently claps. The Africans feel very much "at home" with this custom.

Among the Luo people in Musoma diocese the medicine man has great power and influence. In the local catechesis and local language, explaining Jesus Christ's work as "savior" is very difficult; so he becomes the "Chief Medicine Man" who can cure all the sicknesses and problems of the people. Portraying Jesus as the supreme healer speaks to the Africans' cultural traditions.

The Masai in Arusha diocese are herders. The story of Adam and Eve in the garden and their fall through eating the forbidden fruit has no appeal. In the life-centered African catechesis, Adam and Eve become "Beginner Man" and "Beginner Woman"; the garden becomes a vast plain of animals, and the forbidden fruit becomes the forbidden cow. God, the Creator and Source, permitted our first parents to kill any cow on the plain except the single forbidden cow. When Beginner Man and Beginner Woman slaughtered this cow, they separated themselves from God.

There can be endless variations on the story of creation and the fall. In another ethnic group the story centers on the forbidden yam. Whatever the version, it should relate to the culture, customs, and life situation of the local people.

Parables such as the Good Samaritan, the Prodigal Son, and the Lost Sheep can easily be rooted in local situations. A great devotion to Mary can quickly develop among peoples who give special status to the Queen Mother in their social structure, such as ethnic groups in Uganda.

The emergence of an African Christianity will take time. To nurture it is the responsibility of the African people themselves. This raises serious questions about the role of foreign or expatriate missionaries in Africa today. Are they still needed in Africa (or any other place in the world)? What are their new roles? Bishop Mwoleka feels that foreign missionaries will always have a calling away from their home countries. For an American or European this may mean going to Africa, Asia, or Latin America. For an African missionary this may mean going to another part of Africa or another part of the world. The missionary is a sign of the universal church living and working within the local church.

Contemporary evangelization stresses incarnation, inculturation, and a deeper identification with the local culture and people. The history of missionary activity has produced many models. For all his holiness and zeal, Francis Xavier represents an old model: he preached the gospel to Christianize Asia, "to save souls." More relevant models for contemporary evangelization are Matteo Ricci in China and Robert de Nobili in India. Through their close identification with local culture, traditions, and customs they tried to Asianize Christianity. A twentieth-century model is Charles de Foucauld, who stressed the ministry of spiritual presence in North Africa, living with the local people and sharing deeply in their lives.

Evangelization has been carried out in three ways: (1) *transplantation*: imposing Western expressions of Christianity without modifications; (2) *adaptation*: introducing Western expressions of Christianity with some adjustment to local culture; (3) *incarnation* (inculturation in the best sense of the term): creating truly African expressions of Christianity. This third process has had two recent phases. Initially Western missionaries promoted this task. Now it is clear that only Africans themselves can be the authors of authentic incarnation in their own cultures. Stated another way, missionaries wrote the first chapter of the story of Africanizing Christianity; the second chapter is being written by missionaries and Africans collaborating together. The third and most important chapter will be written by Africans themselves.

What are some contemporary missionary models since the Second Vatican Council? In Asia missionaries are trying to bridge the gap between Western Christianity and Oriental religious thought and practice. Examples are Bede Griffiths, who promotes the merger of the monastic tradition of the West and the tradition of the ashrams in India, and H. M. Enomiya-Lassalle's dialogue with Zen Buddhism in Japan. In Latin America missionaries are identifying with oppressed people in their struggle for liberation, working with basic Christian communities and joining with Christians committed to authentic liberation and social justice. In Africa missionaries are living and sharing with the people on the local level in integrated communities (Western missionaries and Africans living and working together), the ministry of presence in *Ujamaa* villages, and frontier evangelization (missionaries living with nomad groups).

Followers of Charles de Foucauld are inspiring missionary models in many places of the world. The Little Brothers and Little Sisters of Jesus live a spiritual presence among working-class people. The Little Brothers and Little Sisters of the Gospel focus more on the verbal proclamation of the gospel.

Some critics of missionary activity in the contemporary world stress the need for radical changes. They maintain that the imposition of a Western Christ and a Western Christianity on Third World countries can be corrected only by the local churches making a fresh start, free from the trappings and influence of Western Christianity. For the church in Africa this means rediscovering the core of Jesus Christ's saving message and stripping it of various historical and cultural baggage. It means returning to basic gospel values and expressing them anew in the different social and cultural situations of today's world.

This view proposes that the foreign missionary should become like a grain of wheat (John 12:24); the seed has to be buried and "die" before it bears new fruit. At certain times and in certain places (1) the missionary should actually leave a particular country or local area so that the local church can flower in its own way; (2) reduce his or her influence and initiative and become much more a helper of local priests, religious, and lay people; (3) shift to a different workstyle or lifestyle; for example, a ministry of presence rather than an active service ministry.

30-Second Bicycle Ride through the Mind of an African

One Saturday afternoon I was chatting with Thomas, John, and Christopher outside our house in Nyabihanga. Light-heartedly I asked each of them what he would buy if he had 1000 Tanzanian shillings (approximately $140). Thomas said he would buy a transistor radio. (The schoolboys love to listen to pop music from neighboring Burundi and the Tanzania soccer games.) John said he would buy a bicycle, one of the most prized possessions in our village. Christopher thought for a long time and finally said, "If I had a thousand shillings I would buy a cow. I would feed the cow until she got big and fat. Then I would sell the cow for two thousand shillings and go out and buy a transistor radio and a bicycle."

I could identify with Christopher's clever answer. I imagine that there is some tendency toward capitalism in each of us, even in socialistic countries like Tanzania. Yet on many other occasions I could not understand the schoolboys' style of thinking and planning. I remember examples of the boys unexpectedly changing their plans, not arriving at our agreed time, saying yes but meaning no, using my personal goods without asking first. I came to discover, however, that what my Western mind saw as their inconsistency or irresponsibility was my problem, not their problem. I had not really penetrated the rhythm of their African mentality and lifestyle.

To use Western logic in a non-Western culture is a mistake. During a trip I asked a young man named James to buy a carton of milk. He said that it cost three shillings and twenty cents Tanzanian (U.S. $0.47). I gave him a five-shilling note and twenty cents in change in order to get back two shillings without a lot of small change. Immediately James returned the twenty cents, saying he didn't need it, the five shillings would be enough.

Trying to "figure out" Africans by Western standards is a mistake, too. Their spontaneous and "living-for-the-moment" style doesn't fit into our neat categories. Their particular approach to life—synthetic, holistic, and concrete—often enables them to get down to the basics better than most Westerners. Very few Westerners are capable of taking that 30-second bicycle ride through the mind of an African. Gradually I put aside my techniques for analyzing and interpreting Africans. I was happy just to be with them, to share with them, and to try to relate to them from their point of view.

Making the effort to enter into the African point of view gave me a better understanding of Africans themselves and their similarities to and differences from people in other parts of the world. In my experience community and personal relationships are the basic values in life for Africans. Understanding and, more importantly, appreciating these fundamental realities are the key to who the African is, how the person thinks, why the person acts in a certain way, what his or her worldview may be.

Two different examples may make this clear. During a discussion on ways of spending leisure time, Bishop Mwoleka pointed out that many peoples' relaxation is essentially task-oriented—watching television, playing cards, reading a book. The focus is on the activity or the event. Many Africans, however, prefer informally talking with one another—conversation, social get-togethers. The focus is on the personal interaction and the human relations.

The second example took place while a church was being built in the northern part of Rulenge diocese. One of the construction workers did not show up for two days. When he finally arrived at the construction site on the third day, he said that an unexpected visitor had come to his home. When confronted with the choice, he said that he would prefer to lose his job than to neglect his visitor.

This stress on personal relationships has been emphasized by Bishop Albert Yungu of Zaire, who has called urgently for the development of a theology of our fraternity in Christ: "Not only is this truth (all are brothers and sisters, because *filii in Filio*) a specific doctrine of Christianity, but it also finds its sociological and anthropological basis in the African traditions relating to parentage and human relations."

This basic African value of community is even more striking when Africa is compared with other parts of the world. In summarizing the 1974 Synod of Bishops on "Catechesis in Our Time," Brian Hearne stated:

> It became clear that, if the West stood for "truth," Asia for "prayer," Latin America for "liberation," Africa stood for "fraternity." A fundamental value in Africa is that of "sharing," and to share life is the highest value. The mystery of God and of the Trinity can be approached in this way: God, the fullness of life, must also be the fullness of sharing. Human existence is closest to God's (the image and likeness of God) when it is a communication in truth and love. Life in isolation is a contradiction. This even extends to the dead—the "living-dead," the ancestors, who still remain as part of the community, who are still present.

Looking through African eyes to get the African point of view illuminates the "burning issues" of the African church today. To interpret these issues from a Western perspective (using Western culture, standards, and values) is frustrating and unsatisfactory. To appreciate these issues in the context of the African worldview, culture, and society is much more fruitful. Take the issue of structures of ministry, which is controversial in Africa as well as in other parts of the world. Let us approach it not from a Western viewpoint but from an African viewpoint. Christianity in Africa is experiencing the greatest numerical growth on a sustained basis (a seven-and-one-half-million increase of Christians per year) of any continent in any period of history. Archbishop Mark Mihayo of Tanzania has pointed out that 80 percent of the Catholics in Africa are deprived of the Sunday Eucharist and must be satisfied with monthly Eucharist at best. The rapid growth of largely self-ministering SCCs dramatizes the need to provide regular sacramental life and spiritual nourishment on the local level.

So the burning issue is a pastoral one: how to reshape pastoral ministries to serve the spiritual (taken in the wider sense) needs of African Christians. This involves a creative response to different kinds of priests, a variety of lay ministries, and greater pastoral roles for women.

To say there is a shortage of priests in Africa today is not stating the problem accurately. If an increase in local priests merely strengthens the clerical bureaucracy and preferred status of priests, this will mean a perpetuation of the status quo rather than the creative development of African Christianity. The emphasis should not be on the quantity of priests but the quality, especially those who live closer to the people and are open to co-responsibility and team ministry.

Even for the statistical-minded it is clear that the present structures of priestly ministry are inadequate for Africa's pressing pastoral needs. While many African seminaries are full (for example, in Nigeria, Uganda, and Tanzania), and the annual number of ordinations is increasing, the number of Catholics is usually growing much faster proportionately than the number of priests. The one encouraging sign is that in some countries (for example, Kenya) the ratio of Catholics to African priests is decreasing. Recent statistics indicate that there is one priest for every 2500 Catholics in Africa today. Projections indicate that in the year 2000 there will be three times as many priests in Africa, but for every priest there will be 15,000 to 18,000 Catholics.

Consequently, creative pastoral solutions are urgently needed, especially to form and nourish eucharistic communities. Most African bishops are conservative in these matters and reluctant to propose bold changes in the present structure of priestly ministry. Yet a few African bishops have supported the ordination of married men. One type of married priest could be the part-time village priest. He could be the local catechist, or a lay leader in an SCC, who would have less education than a seminary-trained priest.

With a "village church" emerging in rural countries such as Tanzania, ordaining responsible married men who have been selected by the local community is both biblical and realistic. These mature married priests could perform their priestly ministry while being locally self-supporting through farming, a trade, or other work. The village worker-priest would symbolize the integration of the religious and secular spheres, the incarnation of Christianity in contemporary African culture. These village priests would remain at the grassroots level; periodically they would participate in seminars and workshops. They would be part of pastoral teams, including full-time and part-time lay pastoral workers. In their villages these married priests would work with the local leaders of the SCCs, not for them or above them.

Many leaders of the Catholic church in Africa oppose this solution on the ground that it creates second-class priests—a two-level priesthood. Another objection is that village priests would not have a sense of the universal church.

Another type of married priest would be a well-educated, experienced man—a teacher, a civil servant, a professional man. His general educational background would be on the same level as a seminary-educated priest. Such a well-educated married priest could be either part-time or full-time in priestly ministry.

This leaves the sensitive issue of celibacy, which is controversial in Africa as well as in many other parts of the world. In traditional African society everyone marries. Adulthood is intimately connected with the procreation of children. The first-born male has a privileged place. Continuation of the family and clan lineage is imperative. A large family assures the proper veneration of the living-dead.

To many Africans a celibate priest, Brother, Sister, or lay person is an anomaly. Many parents categorically refuse their children permission for any kind of single vocation, although this tradition is changing in third- and fourth-generation Catholic families. For certain African priests celibacy has a specific meaning, that is, not getting married. This does not exclude having a woman quietly on the side and having children.

Celibacy does not have the same value in Africa as it does in many Western countries. This was clearly impressed on me when I asked a Ugandan priest his views on celibacy. He replied by telling a story (a very African way of answering) as an example, not as a general rule. He described a certain Ugandan parish that had two African priests. One priest was hot-tempered and frequently angry. He was often impatient and admonished his parishioners in public. His moral life was entirely proper. The other priest was gentle, kind, and patient. He had a quiet, respectful way of relating to his parishioners. He had difficulty with celibacy and would occasionally lapse. He kept his behavior quiet. When one of these two priests had to be transferred to fill a vacancy in another parish, the local Christian community was consulted. Almost everyone recommended the transfer of the hot-tempered priest.

It is clear that the African church is sharply divided on the celibacy question. Statements of African bishops' conferences regularly support the traditional view on the celibate priesthood. Yet various surveys provide contrasting views. For example, in Zaire, 83 percent of the 595 African priests surveyed favored optional celibacy.

Over the centuries celibacy developed as an ecclesiastical law in the largely Western expansion of Catholicism. Today perhaps another solution is possible for non-Western cultures that have different values attached to celibacy and marriage. Could the African church adopt the practice of the Eastern Rite churches: married priests as well as celibate priests—two charisms evolving out of a particular cultural setting?

A second key issue is marriage, particularly polygamy. Strictly applying Western Christian teachings on marriage to the African situation is highly questionable. Certain African marriage customs are based on deeply human and deeply Christian values— community, sharing, mutual support, strong family ties. The leviratic custom for the care of widows in rural African society has no Western counterpart and deserves special consideration. Christianity (especially its Western forms) should not be imposed on African culture; rather, there should be a blending of the two.

The African church is divided on the polygamy issue. In its recommendations on family life and marriage in 1978, the Symposium of Episcopal Conferences of Africa and Madagascar (SECAM) stated cautiously:

On the one hand, concern is felt to uphold the monogamous ideal of Christian marriage and to give encouragement to those who faithfully live this ideal. . . . On the other hand, compassion is felt for persons who earnestly desire baptism and the sacraments and who have contracted polygamous marriages according to custom and in good faith. Compassion is also felt for Christians who have relapsed into polygamy under social or economic pressures or as a result of childlessness. However, it is also felt that, considering the material at the disposal of the General Assembly, the various pastoral problems connected with marriage in Africa are not yet sufficiently studied as to be ripe for common pastoral solutions on the continental level, especially in view of the different situations existing in different parts of Africa.

Sixteen Christian churches were involved directly or indirectly in the CROMIA (Churches' Research on Marriage in Africa) project which was coordinated by the AMECEA Research Office. The experts in the CROMIA project supported the following position in their report:

Polygamy is a form of marriage that is inferior to monogamy. It is not sinful for non-Christians who follow the custom, and in certain circumstances Christians can tolerate it in order to avoid a greater evil, just as they have tolerated slavery, dictatorships, and other evils in the past.

The report concluded:

The kind of solution that we favor is that practiced by the Lutheran church in Liberia and proposed by the Anglican Consultative Council. It definitely rejects the indiscriminate baptism of polygamists. However, it also assumes that to refuse baptism to polygamists in certain cases is a greater evil than the evil of polygamous marriage itself. The following principles would have to be applied with great care in accordance with local situations:

a. In certain cases people involved in polygamous marriages and in the care of widows according to African custom may be admitted to baptism and the other sacraments.

b. These are exclusively cases of socially approved polygamous marriages.

c. The husband and wives remain in the marriage unions freely and of their own accord.

d. These cases are compassionate exceptions in a community among whom the Christian teaching on monogamy is strictly recognized and lived.

e. These exceptions are made with the explicit consent of the local Christian community as a whole and with the approval of the local church (diocese, country) and its leaders.

f. On the same conditions, Christians who have lapsed into polygamy or into the custom of caring for widows because of social or economic pressure, or the burden of a childless marriage, should be treated with sympathy and even readmitted to Communion if the secondary union cannot be dissolved without hardship or injustice.

A third issue is the self-support, or self-reliance, of the African church, which raises the question of the proper amount of overseas financial aid. Too much money and technical services from abroad can be a disservice rather than a service to the local church in Africa. A dollar generated on the local level is worth five dollars contributed from abroad. One Tanzanian bishop said that he would not begin any new project in his diocese—no matter how good it might be—without a careful plan for continuity and ongoing running expenses and staffing from local resources.

Clear signs point to a gradual reduction in the church's institutional presence in Africa—schools, hospitals, mass-media facilities. The financial burden is too great and the powerful institutional image is ambiguous. As the church's institutional presence becomes smaller, an authentic African Christianity, based on people and not on buildings, has a chance to grow.

There are other burning issues for the African church: social justice and human rights; development vis-à-vis evangelization; urbanization; family life, including premarriage formation, birth control, and strengthening family ties; the growth of the independent churches; the youth apostolate; and the design of seminary training. The basic issue would seem to be how to deepen the quality of the Christian life in Africa today. The Second Vatican Council's *Decree on the Missionary Activity of the Church* explains the church's goal as "full participation in the Mystery of Christ." How can this be achieved through the development of an authentic African Christianity?

Forming and deepening SCCs is certainly one meaningful way. As Christian communities build on the community values of African society, one of Bishop Mwoleka's insights is that these African values can be both an asset and a liability. Africans emphasize personal relationships and the importance of maintaining harmony and fraternity above everything else. Yet this can lead to superficial agreement and even an appeasement mentality at the expense of deeper sharing. In his plan for integrated communities (priest, religious, and lay people, married and single, old and young) Bishop Mwoleka feels that only Christian fraternal correction—speaking the truth in love (Eph. 4:25)—will enable people to grow in the Christian life. As community members open their hearts to each other and receive both constructive criticism and affirmation, Christian community develops through the mutual support of the integrated communities. Thus Mwoleka challenges African Christians to live out deep gospel values that sometimes go counter to certain values of the African culture.

VI
Our Journeys Continue

Saying goodbye to my friend Renerida, the daughter of the new catechist Domitian, is very hard. The African way is to say "goodbye until we meet again." An African proverb says "that which is good is never finished."

Father Edward Farrell and St. Agnes parishioners are creating small Christian community zones in Detroit's inner-city. They are discovering that African Christian values are universal Christian values that speak to black parishes in the United States.

Members of the small Christian community zones in St. Agnes Parish in Detroit perform a dramatic reading of the African play "The Unsurpassed Great Spirit" during their eight-day mission retreat. The community zones foster black Christian values such as sharing, hospitality, and service.

The End That Was
a New Beginning

It was two o'clock on a hot August afternoon in 1978 at Rusumo, the border control between Tanzania and Rwanda, and I was leaving Africa. Five Tanzanian friends from Nyabihanga and Bukiriro villages had accompanied me to the border to say goodbye and wish me a safe journey back to America. Two of them, Athanasius and Thomas, had got up at 4:30 A.M. to walk eight miles to Rulenge where they could get a ride to the border.

There at Rusumo under the hot tropical sun my friends asked for a final blessing. I prayed for them and for all the people of Nyabihanga and Bukiriro villages, especially for the Christian community. Earlier, Athanasius had prayed "for our Father Joseph, that he will continue to love us and pray for us while he is away." Then we said, "Kwa heri ya kuonana," which is Swahili for "goodbye until we meet again."

So I left Tanzania after ten years in Africa, the last two spent with the people in Nyabihanga. But my journey in life continued—both the outward journey of a traveler and the inner journey of a pilgrim. Because of a new assignment in America, I knew I would be away from Tanzania for at least three years. But sometime, somehow, I would return.

On the previous Sunday we had walked from Nyabihanga village to Bukiriro village for a farewell Eucharist at Bukiriro outstation, where we had celebrated the Eucharist on many Sundays during the past two years. An early morning mist clung to the tropical land, and the fierce African sun seemed reluctant to wake up to begin a new day. There was even the threat of a shower in what was the middle of the traditional dry season. We were uncertain whether to have the Eucharist inside the church or outside. In the end we celebrated the Eucharist inside the packed church, while those who could not find room stood patiently outside in the hot sun.

In the farewell homily I used two African proverbs to express my feelings about leaving our Christian community after sharing so deeply for two full years: "Mountains never meet but people do," an optimistic way of saying that we would meet again, that someday I would return to Tanzania. The second proverb was "A reserve does not decay," emphasizing the importance of having more volunteers trained to teach religion in our primary schools and in our Sunday school, and more prayer leaders trained for our weekly Bible services.

Since animating SCCs had been my main pastoral work during my two years in the outstation, I used a Swahili saying meaning "Unity is strength" to emphasize the development of our eucharistic community, a thought that was reiterated in the Eucharistic Prayer: "May all of us who share in the body and blood of Christ be brought together in the unity of the Holy Spirit."

After the Eucharist, the Christians sang and performed traditional dances of the Washubi people. Four members of the choir recited a "Poem of Farewell" as a goodbye not only to me, but also to four leaders of the Bukiriro outstation who were going to Munich, West Germany, to learn new approaches to forming SCCs. I had worked closely with these leaders for two years so I felt moved that the local Christian community was saying goodbye to us as a group. We were missionaries being sent out by the local church of Bukiriro.

Before my final leavetaking, I boldly asked for a gift. Not a gift of the harvest or of the local cultural handicraft. Not a material gift. Not something that could be bought. I asked for the gift of the continuing growth and deepening of our Christian community in Bukiriro outstation. I told my friends that I could receive this gift only later on—six months, a year, perhaps two years later. The gift would come when the Christian leaders would write to me in America about the continuing growth of our outstation: about our SCCs continuing to pray together and help needy people; about the Christians showing concrete signs of love, sharing, and service; about the expansion of our church farm and church forest so that the community could achieve complete self-reliance; and about an increasing number of young people getting married in church. Receiving news of these "happenings" would be the greatest gift of all.

In turn, I wanted to leave a gift for the Christians of Bukiriro outstation. I told them that my most precious possession was my chalice, a gift from my parents at my ordination in 1966. I explained that leaving my chalice for the Christians—for other priests to use during the Sunday Eucharist—was a way for me to remain a part of their eucharistic community. In the Eucharist we would always be linked to Christ and to each other and we would always pray for one another.

Then we ate together—cooked bananas, goat meat, and banana beer. The people are very poor and hardly ever eat meat, but on this occasion they insisted on using most of the money in their small treasury to buy a goat for the celebration. After the meal there were short talks emphasizing that we were saying farewell but not goodbye. Sometime we would meet again.

One man mentioned the proverb, "Relationship is in the eating together." In the African tradition personal relationships are deepened by eating a meal together, a sign of unity and sharing. He applied the proverb to Christ and his disciples; then to the Christian community at Bukiriro itself. He said that our relationship with Christ and with each other is deepened when we partake of his body and blood in the Eucharist. He linked the celebration of the Eucharist with our festive meal, stressing the African values of community and sharing.

Late Sunday afternoon the SCC of Nyabuliga (the section of Nyabihanga where we lived) hosted a beer party to say goodbye. This was the Washubi people's best and most traditional way of saying farewell. Over 125 people, Christians and members of African traditional religions alike, came to drink millet beer prepared by our neighbors.

Afterward members of the Nyabuliga SCC Prayer Group gathered for songs and speeches at the house of the African Sisters. A young Christian leader read an official "Message of Farewell." With community treasury funds the leaders bought a locally-made basket, which they presented while the following part of the farewell message was read:

From the sale of part of the harvest of the community field, Nyabuliga Small Christian Community has given Father Joseph a handmade gift according to the local culture and customs. May it remind him and his friends of Nyabuliga. When he reaches America may it be a token of our gratitude for his work in our small Christian community of which he was such a real part.

On Monday morning we celebrated the Eucharist for the last time in Nyabihanga. The First Reading was the end of Saint Paul's Letter to the Philippians when he says goodbye to his most beloved Christian community: "I miss you very much, dear friends; you are my joy and my crown" (Phil. 4:1). The Gospel was the end of Saint Mark's Gospel, where our Lord commissioned his disciples to "go out to the whole world, proclaim the Good News to all creation" (16:16).

Just as Saint Paul did in his day, I felt a mixture of joy and sadness at leaving the Christian community: joy at experiencing the growth of our SCCs in the Bukiriro outstation; sadness at leaving close friends and a loving, sharing community. Like the first apostles, I realized that the missionary call is a call to go forth continually, and to respond to the needs of new people, new places, and new situations.

For our last breakfast the African Sisters cooked the eggs the people had given us. Throughout the morning villagers dropped in to say farewell. Then, after lunch, an African priest drove me to Rulenge. In accordance with the African custom of escorting departing friends part way on their journey, two African Sisters and two of the Christian leaders accompanied us. The following morning we drove another forty-two miles to the border.

There at the Tanzanian border I did not feel that I had left behind my five friends, or Nyabihanga, or Tanzania. In a very real way I felt that part of me remained there with my friends, and part of them came away with me; leaving was not the end—only the end that was a new beginning. Although separated by eight thousand miles, I would be united in many ways with my Nyabihanga community. What I had discovered and learned and shared in Africa would always be a part of me and part of my missionary journey wherever I would be and wherever I would go.

Our Journeys Continue

Since leaving Tanzania I have received many touching letters. A close friend in Nyabihanga thanks me for "embracing the life of us Africans at its roots." A couple very close to me referred to the desire "to live and share the lot of the African people at the grassroots level—in an *Ujamaa* village in Tanzania. We know the experience (whatever problems and difficulties you might have experienced) have made you much closer to the heart and spirit of Africa."

The most meaningful letters came from Christians in Nyabihanga and Bukiriro describing how our Christian community continued to pray together, to work together, and to grow. Every departing missionary has similar concerns and questions: When I leave how will the local Christians get along? Will the pastoral work we started continue? How will the local church develop? During the first few weeks after leaving the village I often wondered what the first letters would say. Who had had a baby? Who had died recently? Were the SCCs still meeting regularly? Were our new lay leaders fulfilling their pastoral responsibilities? Did the Christians continue to carry water to the church to make bricks? Was the weekly practical action to help the poor and needy continuing? An earlier comment that without a resident priest and the lay leaders who had gone to West Germany our outstation would go backward still bothered me, but I felt confident that the Holy Spirit would be with our Christians, especially in the SCCs.

During our last evening together in Nyabihanga we had joked about who would be the first to write. Athanasius Misambo promised that he would be the first. Sister Veronica said she would be the first. I arrived at my home in Baltimore during the first week of October, exactly two months after leaving Nyabihanga. As I flipped through the mail I saw two blue airforms with Tanzanian stamps. I eagerly opened them. One letter was from Athanasius, the other from Sister Veronica. Both had won!

The two letters described all the local news in our village and outstation. One of our friendliest neighbors, Emmanuel, had died suddenly. Nyabuliga SCC conducted a special prayer service and helped his children. The extension of the Bukiriro church was almost finished; the tin roof would be up before the beginning of the rainy season. All the SCCs except Rubanga were meeting regularly. Many Christians were participating in the Sunday Eucharist. I was elated.

Over the next few months I continued to get news regularly. Our new prayer leader, Privatus Sentore, wrote in a typical African style that combined optimism and pessimism: "All the small Christian communities are continuing well but difficulties still enter in." He mentioned positive signs such as the large attendance of SCC prayer leaders at monthly meetings and the motivation of the children during Sunday school, but he also mentioned disappointing signs such as certain Christians shortening the Bible services and other Christians refusing to attend Bible services if it meant a long walk.

Even some of the "bad news" was good news to me. The retired catechist Salvatori wrote that the church walls had not been enlarged enough. On the biggest feasts Christians still had to stand outside.

Some of the priests in Rulenge diocese were skeptical about the lay Christians of Bukiriro managing on a regular basis without a priest. They had seen many outstations lose their enthusiasm after a period of time. Yet after ten months one priest wrote me:

> Last Sunday I went to Bukiriro for Corpus Christi. There was a big crowd of people, more than 165 communions, a very nice procession without any disturbance. I came back happy. We really saw the result of the apostolate of these last two years. This outstation is surely far different from the others.

Other letters were less encouraging. While the SCCs continued to pray and work together, the Bernadette Sisters had to animate the Christians regularly. The joint church farm had gone down because some SCCs failed to do their share of the work.

In general, however, there has been progress and momentum in Bukiriro outstation. Astheria Ngenzi attributed this success to our building a strong, solid foundation in 1977 and 1978. Now the Christian community is adding to this basic foundation.

As I reflected on these letters from Nyabihanga and Bukiriro I realized that all of us are on unique journeys in life—understood fully by God alone. I like to think of three kinds of journeys: the journey of the African people; the journey of you, the reader; my own journey.

The African people have a special journey. For many, especially those in southern Africa, it is still a journey toward freedom and independence. For many others, especially those oppressed by dictators, military regimes, and tribalism, it is a journey toward social justice, social equality, and basic human rights. For many, many others it is a journey toward fulfilling basic human needs such as food, clothing, housing, health care, and education. The African peoples' rendezvous with destiny is filled with both excitement and uncertainty. May it lead to peace, social and economic development, and a deepening of genuine African life.

The African church has a journey to become a truly local church: self-supporting, self-ministering, and self-propagating. The quest for an authentic African Christianity will be long and slow. It means discovering and rediscovering African Christian values that are relevant for our contemporary world. The road ahead includes the development of African theology, new forms of ministry, and stronger foundations for the SCCs.

The journey continues for the people of Nyabihanga and Bukiriro: for village leaders such as Nchabukoroka, Patrice, Richard; for full-time pastoral workers such as Bishop Christopher, the Bernadette Sisters, and Astheria; for lay leaders of the Christian community such as Athanasius, Petro, Salvatori, Privatus, Theresa, and Angelo; for young people such as Thomas, John, Christopher, and Gaudensia; for children such as Angelina, Mathias, and Chiza. Seeds of hope are being planted in the village fields to produce a better material life. Seeds of hope are being planted in the hearts of the village men, women, and children to produce lives of sharing, love, and service.

I invite each reader—whoever you are, wherever you live, whatever you do—to continue your own special journey after you finish reading this book. If you are a missionary, I hope your journey will enable you to fall in love with, and become one with, the people and culture you serve. If you are a black Christian, I hope your journey will enable you to understand and appreciate better your African Christian roots. If you are an African, I hope your journey will enable you to develop an authentic African Christianity. If you are a person interested in Africa, I hope your journey will enable you to understand and appreciate better the spirit and character of the African people. If you are a concerned Christian in Western society—a teacher, a housewife, a pastoral worker, a social activist, a contemplative—I hope your journey will enable you to reach out to all peoples and cultures. If you are a person concerned with rediscovering human and spiritual values I hope your journey will enable you to integrate African Christian values in your own life.

What of my own journey? As I write this I am beginning a new three-year assignment in spiritual formation in America. My missionary journey continues in a new way, helping to prepare future overseas missionaries. Although I have temporarily left Africa in one way, in another way I can never leave Africa. I can never forget the people of Nyabihanga, of Tanzania, of Africa. I carry the people of Africa, especially my friends in the village, in my heart wherever I go. The African people have enriched and inspired me in countless ways.

The first step in leaving the village is the beginning of a long journey to return. I pray for the strength and courage to be faithful to the African people and the African dream. I especially pray to be faithful to the parting words of a close friend: "As you return to your country, the United States, please carry Africa with you in your heart. May you serve as a living bridge between your people and those of Africa."

As our journeys continue, African Christian values such as community, personal relationships, fraternity, the extended family, sharing, respect for old age, hospitality, patience, simplicity, and service to the community challenge us to live more deeply human and more deeply Christian lives. As an African would say, we really don't travel alone; we make the journey together.

Journey from Tanzania to Detroit

One year and a half after returning to the United States I flew to Detroit, Michigan, to conduct a mission retreat in St. Agnes, a predominantly black parish in the inner city. Our theme was "Experiencing African Christian Values." About our eight days of shared prayer, talks, audio-visual presentations (including movies and slides), small-group discussions, and social involvement in the local community, one of the black parishioners wrote me:

> I thank you for bringing us "the African Way." It is very beautiful and is filled with deep human understanding. I always feel a spirit of kinship when I see a film of Africa. It is as if I were there; as if it is a part of me that is forever latent.

I felt completely at home in the black community in Detroit—just as I had felt one with the African people in Tanzania. I was returning to my own roots, since I was born in St. Agnes Parish forty-two years before, then moved to the east coast after a few months. Now I was helping black Catholics to get in touch with their African roots.

During the mission retreat we had a talk and an audio-visual show for senior citizens every morning and a similar presentation followed by an hour of discussion every evening for all the parishioners. From 8 to 9 A.M. the St. Agnes pastoral team met for prayer and reflection. The noon Eucharist focused on the theme of the day, using special readings and African Eucharistic Prayers. Each theme embraced an African Christian value with a universal meaning: community, waiting, familyhood, sharing, joint responsibility, faith, self-determination, and call to unity in action. For each theme there was a Swahili code word (for example, *jumuiya* for "community"), a short African story, an African proverb, a relevant Bible reading, and suggestions for concrete action such as sharing with neighbors and helping needy persons in the community. A display of African art, Bible pictures, local clothes and vestments, and photographs from Nyabihanga village provided an African setting in the back of the church.

Most of the themes relate to Kwanza, a program for developing black consciousness and heritage in the United States as part of the celebration of the firstfruits of African harvest festivals. (*Kwanza* is the Swahili word for first.) St. Agnes and other parishes and schools in Detroit are using Kwanza to celebrate our African heritage, to give thanks to our ancestors, and to reinforce the black value system, which is closely related to gospel values.

Twenty-five years ago St. Agnes was a middle-class white parish with several thousand Catholic families. As the whites moved into the suburbs the blacks moved into the inner city. The 1967 riots in Detroit left the neighborhood scarred with burned-out buildings and alienated hearts. In 1978 the pastor, Father Ed Farrell, began a new program of evangelization and outreach. He formed a pastoral team composed of five white Sisters, a black minister of service (similar to a permanent deacon), a retired black Internal Revenue Service worker, and two Irish lay volunteers. Inspired by the success of SCCs in Africa and other places in the world, the team divided the mile-square St. Agnes Parish into seven zones, or SCCs. The parish became a communion of seven SCCs and each community a neighborhood of families. The parish's pastoral plan stresses grassroots urban evangelization.

St. Agnes is really a mission situation. There are only one hundred Catholic families in a total population of 20,000 people. Only ten families are intact, that is, father, mother, and children living together. Young people are few and the committed ones even fewer. Crime and violence abound. The inner city breeds fear, distrust, and individualism—not a likely place for neighborhood SCCs to flourish.

This was the setting for our mission retreat—the first one in St. Agnes in fifteen years. The presentation of African Christian values produced a wide spectrum of reactions and feelings. Many black Catholics were happy to rediscover African values that have meaning in contemporary urban America. Middle-aged blacks who had migrated to Detroit from the south fondly remembered their southern heritage. For some persons in this same group our African focus only brought painful memories of years gone by. Many black Detroiters recognized themselves and their urban subculture in the African values of extended family bonds, waiting, hospitality, and sharing as a way of life. Others didn't see the relevance of their romanticized "primitive" African past and challenged Tanzanians to break out of their endless circle of poverty, low standard of living, and lack of initiative. Some of the best-educated blacks considered the return to African roots to be a step backward. They stressed that their roots are in American history and culture, not in a romanticized Africa.

In this setting of mixed attitudes and feelings we searched and explored together. Our reflections on many African Christian values concluded that they are universal Christian values that are expressed in African society and culture as well as other societies and cultures. As the mission retreat progressed we asked how these values could be expressed in a Western capitalistic society, in the inner city of Detroit, in the neighborhoods and apartment houses in St. Agnes Parish. During the small-group meetings of the SCCs, the zone participants reflected about the waiting ministry on the street corners of Detroit, or the hospitality in welcoming a visitor to a potluck communal meal in the parish auditorium after the Sunday Eucharist, or visiting elderly shut-ins in a nearby nursing home.

As the reflections moved deeper the participants concluded that many times Christians are called to be countercultural in contemporary society. To live truly gospel values of community, sharing, and joint responsibility we have to swim against the tide of American consumerism, individualism, and intense competition. Gradually the parishioners in the mission retreat identified specific St. Agnes Parish Christian values—universal values that have special meaning in their lives. Examples are *risk* and *outreach*. Christians in Detroit's inner city are challenged to overcome the fear, suspicion, and alienation in their neighborhoods. This means being vulnerable to others—opening our homes to visitors, including needy strangers, telephoning a lonely person after we have been rebuffed, giving rides to travelers late at night. This outreach is also expressed through service to the needy and the wider community: visiting shut-ins, preparing goodwill bags for poor families, and sharing with persons in the community who are out of work.

During the mission retreat a key insight was the importance of a community response. Risk and outreach are not just personal responsibilities but the joint action of the seven SCC zones and the whole parish. Zone I Christians supported one of its members in a protest against the negligence of a slum landlord. Zone VII members decided to prepare Christmas gifts for needy families in their neighborhood.

At the end of our mission retreat, the seven SCC zones started concrete follow-up. Several zones decided to meet weekly in their neighborhood groups for prayer, discussion, and informal sharing together. Others planned specific social action to help the sick, mentally retarded, and lonely. Zone I leader Tom Grove said that the zone members wanted to put into practice the African saying that "Christianity is living for others." Inez Jenkins, the leader of Zone IV, decided to link her SCC with an SCC in Nyabihanga. She wrote Thomas Kidende, one of the Tanzanian lay leaders, and suggested this twinning plan. Thus a black Christian community in Detroit's inner city joined hands with an African Christian community in rural western Tanzania.

Like my other journeys, my journey to Detroit became a pilgrimage of discovery and sharing. During our mission retreat I learned an African proverb from one of the participants that speaks to all human experience whether the place be Africa or America or somewhere else: "I am because we are; we are because I am."

The last slide during our closing Eucharist describes this in another way. It is a picture of four hands—black, white, red, and yellow—clasped together in unity. As for the participants in our mission retreat, this has a priceless message for all humankind. We are united to one another—brothers and sisters in the human family, God's people. We travel the same road together.

Index

African Christianity, xvi, 37-38,
108, 141, 158, 166-76, 179,
183-84, 194-95
African Christian Spirituality,
140-49
African Eucharistic Prayers,
146-48, 169, 196
African sayings, 29, 33, 127, 134,
139, 172, 189, 195, 199
African Traditional Religions,
25-30, 43, 58-60, 108, 118, 122,
140-48, 173, 190
AMECEA (Association of Member Episcopal Conferences in
Eastern Africa), 8-9, 24, 32,
38, 168, 170-71, 182
Ancestors (living-dead), 30, 47,
141-42, 144-48, 161, 178,
180,196

Bible, 5, 9, 14, 47-48, 59, 67, 71,
78, 87, 90-91, 99-100, 125-28,
130, 132, 134, 176, 184, 191
Black Christ, 169-71

Common work, 25, 32, 62-68, 81,
91, 139
Community, xvi, 9-12, 15, 17, 22,
24, 30, 34-43, 46, 48-51, 58-61,
62-63, 66, 68, 70, 72, 75-77, 79,
86-87, 94, 98-149, 159-60, 163,
165, 167, 171, 177-81, 183-84,
188-93, 195-99

Contemplation, 9-12, 24, 73-74,
78, 103-8, 142-43, 195
Conversion, 7, 22, 111

Dancing, 92, 136, 140, 144, 162,
169, 171, 189
Death, 27-31, 61, 121, 125, 128,
131, 134, 141-42, 144-48, 161,
164
de Foucauld, Brother Charles, 8,
71, 174-75

Ecumenism, 26, 43
Escorting, 164-66, 188, 191
Extended family, 33, 62, 109, 142,
195, 197

Fifth Gospel, xvi, 129
Fraternity, 142, 178, 184, 195
Friendship, 26, 33-34, 36, 45, 50,
103-4, 126, 142, 157, 189, 192

Gospel values, 10, 17, 24, 47-49,
67, 78, 91, 100-01, 106, 109,
120, 144, 171, 176, 184, 197-98
Greeting, 18, 32-33, 35, 80, 136,
142, 154, 157-59

Hospitality, 32-34, 36, 92, 101,
110, 140, 165, 195-98

Incarnation, 72, 78-79, 143, 146,
149, 166-76, 180

201

Photo Credits

OTHER ORBIS TITLES

ANDERSON, Gerald H.
ASIAN VOICES IN CHRISTIAN THEOLOGY

"Anderson's book is one of the best resource books on the market that deals with the contemporary status of the Christian church in Asia. After an excellent introduction, nine scholars, all well-known Christian leaders, present original papers assessing the theological situation in (and from the viewpoint of) their individual countries. After presenting a brief historical survey of the development of the Christian church in his country, each author discusses 'what is being done by the theologians there to articulate the Christian message in terms that are faithful to the biblical revelation, meaningful to their cultural traditions, and informed concerning the secular movements and ideologies.' An appendix (over 50 pages) includes confessions, creeds, constitutions of the churches in Asia. Acquaintance with these original documents is imperative for anyone interested in contemporary Asian Christian theology." *Choice*

ISBN 0-88344-017-2   *Cloth $15.00*
ISBN 0-88344-016-4   *Paper $7.95*

APPIAH-KUBI, Kofi & Sergio Torres
AFRICAN THEOLOGY EN ROUTE

Papers from the Pan-African Conference of Third World Theologians, Accra, Ghana.

"If you want to know what 17 Africans are thinking theologically today, here is the book to check." *Evangelical Missions Quarterly*

"Gives us a wonderful insight into the religious problems of Africa and therefore is well worth reading." *Best Sellers*

"This collection of presentations made at the 1977 Conference of Third World Theologians reveals not a finished product but, as the title suggests, a process. . . .On the whole, the book is well written and, where necessary, well translated. It adds to a growing literature on the subject and is recommended for libraries seriously concerned with theology in Africa." *Choice*

ISBN 0-88344-010-5   *184pp. Paper $7.95*

CAMARA, Dom Helder
THE DESERT IS FERTILE

"Dom Helder Camara of Brazil, is a Roman Catholic archbishop whose sense of God's presence breathes through every page. But there is a difference. For Dom Helder has found God's presence in the lives of the poor, in the voices of the oppressed, and he communicates this sense of God's reality very powerfully. He takes us on a spiritual journey that can be utterly transforming if we will risk opening ourselves to him. He is no pessimist; in a world that seems devoid of God's presence, Dom Helder insists that *The Desert Is Fertile*. He does not minimize the 'desert' quality of modern existence: the increasing gap between rich and poor, the insanity of the arms race, and the 'marginalization' of human life, by which he means our tendency to treat the majority of the human family as nonpersons, those who are pushed over to the edges of life and ignored. 'The scandal of this century,' he writes, 'is marginalization.' He reminds us that if to have too little is a problem, so is having too much. 'Poverty makes people subhuman. Excess of wealth makes people inhuman.'" *Christianity and Crisis*

ISBN 0-88344-078-4   *75pp. Cloth $3.95*

CARDENAL, Ernesto
THE GOSPEL IN SOLENTINAME   I

"Farmers and fishermen in a remote village in Nicaragua join their priest for dialogues on Bible verses. The dialoguers discover Jesus as the liberator come to deliver *them* from oppression, inequality, and injustice imposed by a rich, exploitive class: they identify Herod as dictator Somoza. Their vision of the Kingdom of God on earth impels them toward political revolution. This is 'Marxian Christianity' not as abstract theory but gropingly, movingly articulated by poor people. Highly recommended to confront the complacent with the stark realities of religious and political consciousness in the Third World." *Library Journal*

ISBN 0-88344-170-5   *Paper $4.95*

THE GOSPEL IN SOLENTINAME II

"Volume 2 follows the pattern of the first volume: villagers in Nicaragua join their priest, Ernesto, in interpreting New Testament verses. These volumes offer a profound challenge to the Christian conscience, and insight into the recent uprisings in Nicaragua. Highly recommended." *Library Journal*

ISBN 0-88344-167-5   *Cloth $6.95*

THE GOSPEL IN SOLENTINAME III

"A continuation of guided discussions on Gospel passages by the peasant folks in the Central American village of Solentiname. Has a most refreshing outlook." *The Priest*

Fortunately, the manuscripts for this and the fourth volume were safely in Orbis' hands before Somoza's soldiers destroyed Solentiname.

ISBN 0-88344-172-1   *320pp. Cloth $7.95*

FABELLA, Virginia, M.M. & Sergio Torres
THE EMERGENT GOSPEL
Theology from the Underside of History

"*The Emergent Gospel*, I believe, is an expression of a powerful and barely noticed movement. It is the report of an ecumenical conference of 22 theologians from Africa, Asia and Latin America, along with one representative of black North America, who met in Dar es Salaam, Tanzania, in August 1976. Their objective was to chart a new course in theology, one that would reflect the view 'from the underside of history,' that is, from the perspective of the poor and marginalized peoples of the world. Precisely this massive shift in Christian consciousness is the key to the historical importance of the meeting. The majority of the essays were written by Africans, a smaller number by Asians and, surprisingly, only three by Latin Americans, who thus far have provided the leadership in theology from the developing world." *America*

ISBN 0-88344-112-8
Cloth $12.95

FENTON, Thomas P.
EDUCATION FOR JUSTICE: A RESOURCE MANUAL

"The completeness of the source material on the topic and the adaptability of the methodology—stressing experiential education—to groups at the high school, college, or adult levels make this manual a time and energy saving boon for most anyone having to work up a syllabus on 'justice.' This manual would be a worthwhile addition to any religion and/or social studies curriculum library." *Review for Religious*

"The resource volume is rich in ideas for a methodology of teaching Christian justice, and in identifying the problems. It is also very rich in the quality of the background readings provided. The participant's volume is a catchy workbook with many illustrations. It encourages the student (young or adult) to look at the problems as they are experienced by real live persons." *The Priest*

"Replete with background essays, tested group exercises, course outlines and annotated bibliography, this manual should give any teacher or seminar leader plenty of material to launch a thorough study program—and plenty of strongly stated positions for students to react to." *America*

ISBN 0-88344-154-3   *Resource Manual $7.95*
ISBN 0-88344-120-9   *Participant Workbook $3.95*

GUTIERREZ, Gustavo
A THEOLOGY OF LIBERATION
Selected by the reviewers of *Christian Century* as one of the twelve religious books published in the 1970s which "most deserve to survive."

"Rarely does one find such a happy fusion of gospel content and contemporary relevance." *The Lutheran Standard*

ISBN 0-88344-477-1   *Cloth $7.95*
ISBN 0-88344-478-X   *Paper $4.95*

RAYAN, Samuel

THE HOLY SPIRIT
Heart of the Gospel and Christian Hope

"*The Holy Spirit* by Samuel Rayan, an important Indian theologian, gives a bold interpretation of the New Testament and of the central role of the Holy Spirit, a role which western Christianity has often neglected." *Cross Currents*

"This work has a freshness and vitality that is captivating and thought-provoking. It should be read slowly because Rayan speaks truth so simply and beautifully that I found my reading moving easily to reflection and prayer. It is a book not to be easily forgotten because it so well integrates the action of the Spirit with the call to do justice in the world. I hope it will have wide circulation since it can easily be a source for personal spiritual growth, a teaching resource for prayer communities and parish education groups, and a means of formation of Christian leaders." *Catholic Charismatic*

ISBN 0-88344-188-8   *Paper $5.95*

REILLY, Michael Collins, S.J.

SPIRITUALITY FOR MISSION
Historical, Theological, and Cultural Factors for a Present-Day Missionary Spirituality

"Reilly's thesis is that, since the nature of missionary work has changed in recent years and since the theology of mission is now in a state of development, the motivation and spirituality for the modern missionary must also change. *Spirituality for Mission* synthesizes much of the current discussion on mission work and the concerns related to missionary work. Much recent literature deals with missions, but the significance of this book is that it treats the person who is involved in missionary work. It sets forth the importance and value of the missionary vocation." *Theological Studies*

"The book is a rich one. Reilly's statements on evangelization and development, on the aims of mission, and other questions are clearer than many other statements published in recent years." *Philippine Studies*

ISBN 0-88344-464-X   *Paper $8.95*